THE TRUTH ABOUT
Handguns

D1557431

Exploding the Myths, Hype, and Misinformation

Duane Thomas

Paladin Press • Boulder, Colorado

The Truth about Handguns: Exploding the Myths,
  Hype, and Misinformation
by Duane Thomas

Copyright © 1997 by Duane Thomas
ISBN 0-87364-953-2
Printed in the United States of America

Published by Paladin Press, a division of
Paladin Enterprises, Inc.
Gunbarrel Tech Center
7077 Winchester Circle
Boulder, Colorado 80301 USA
+1.303.443.7250

Direct inquiries and/or orders to the above address.

PALADIN, PALADIN PRESS, and the "horse head" design
are trademarks belonging to Paladin Enterprises and
registered in United States Patent and Trademark Office.

Visit our Web site at www.paladin-press.com

T A B L E   O F

CONTENTS

SO MANY MYTHS, SO LITTLE TIME

Have no respect whatsoever for authority; forget who said it and instead look at what he starts with, where he ends up, and ask yourself, "Is it reasonable?"

—Richard Feynman
from his father

There is an incredible amount of hokum, nonsense, and utter garbage that is held up as solemn truth in the world of the handgun. In this book I'm going to address many of the common myths to which I've been exposed during my years in the gun world.

Let's get one myth out of the way right off the bat: I make my living as a professional free-lance gunwriter. You may have heard the persistent rumors that, once you become well established in the gunwriting community, you'll be able to call up all the major gun companies and have them send you pretty much anything you want to play with, ammo companies will send you umpteen thousand rounds of free ammunition, famous firearms instructors will extend you offers to attend their training gratis if only you'll write it up, the finest pistolsmiths in the nation will line up to work on your guns for free, and you'll find yourself sleeping with beautiful gun groupies. Well, I'm here to tell you from firsthand experience . . . *it's all true!*

That being the case, I've had the opportunity, since I assumed the dubious profession of gunwriter, to pour an enormous number of rounds (consisting of just about every type of ammo out there) through any handgun that's caught my fancy. I've been able to wring these firearms out, at leisure and in depth, to ferret out their strong and weak points, to find out what works and what doesn't. In the past three years I've attended approximately 20 high-level firearms training classes, most of them relating to the defensive handgun, in the process becomin' a not-half-bad pistol shot. What's more, while researching my articles I've been afforded the great and luxurious privilege of being able to pick the brains of the most knowledgeable combat trainers and gunsmiths in America, at length. (The beautiful women are none of your business.) And what I learned while doing all that was that much of the "wisdom" that is common coin in the gun community just ain't necessarily so.

I've always been the sort of person who hates relying on hearsay in any area that really matters to me (just call me Doubting Thomas). "What are the facts," I ask myself. Don't give me unsubstantiated rumors, dogma, prejudice, statements everyone "just knows" are true. Again and again and again, what are the facts! I want to *know* . . . and until you test something out for yourself, you *don't* know; you're just taking someone else's word for it.

From that mind-set, and those experiences, comes the gist of this book. Travel with me for awhile as we examine:

- many of the myths surrounding "The King of Combat Handguns," the Colt .45 auto
- the real deal on those pesky and impossible-to-shoot double-action (DA) autos
- handgun stopping power
- the truth about Alvin York's incredible World War I firefight
- the arguments both for and against the high-capacity auto pistol and how that relates to the ideal of the "one-shot stop"
- the answers to the questions, "Are revolvers dead?" and "Just how good is the .40 Smith & Wesson cartridge?"
- some common attitudes toward handguns that I feel are based more on emotion than logic

- and, finally, we'll end on a light note as we take a little trip through the world of handgun trivia

Let's get this show on the road!

CHAPTER ONE

THE KING OF COMBAT HANDGUNS

You should not have a favorite weapon. To become over-familiar with one weapon is as much a fault as not knowing it sufficiently well.

—Miyamoto Mushashi
A Book of Five Rings

A disproportionate number of the insubstantial myths in the field of defensive handgun usage are propounded by devotees of the 1911 auto, aka the Colt .45. I find this sad, because the 1911 is such a good gun—there are enough logical real-world reasons to like it that there's no need for such fatuous reasoning (and large amounts of hot air) to justify its popularity. Be that as it may, here are some of the silly statements I've heard or read about the Colt .45 auto during my years of dealing with firearms on a daily basis:

"Single-action autos like the Colt .45 and the Browning Hi-Power have real-world battle records light-years beyond any other designs. This proves they're the best fighting handguns around."

No. This proves that handguns are considered almost worthless as fighting tools in real wars, and since the Colt .45 and Browning Hi-Power tended to work acceptably well, for decades it wasn't worth the money it would've cost to test and reequip with new examples of such nearly useless weapons.

We might pause to ask ourselves, just *who* says handguns are almost worthless in real wars? Duane Thomas by his lonesome? Answer: The folks who decide where the money goes to upgrade and replace weapons systems, that's who. I'm not saying I personally believe that handguns are *always* worthless in battle; the experiences of the American York in World War I France and the South African van Vuuren in Angola show us this is not the case. However, York only went to his .45 because he found himself with a partially loaded five-shot bolt-action rifle facing six charging men. Had he been armed with a higher-capacity and faster-firing rifle he would have stuck with it over the handgun, as would anyone with a higher-than-room-temperature IQ. Similarly, van Vuuren was an armored car commander, and such troops are not issued long guns because the tight confines of their fighting vehicles make the use of such bulky weapons extremely difficult.

But in the modern battlefield, just how frequently do feats of handgun marksmanship like York's and van Vuuren's occur? Not very damned often. It's not that handguns are *never* of any use in war but that the armies of the world (with justification) consider them of minimal use, at best. Therefore, the fact that the P35 and 1911 stayed standard issue for so long merely indicates that most armies consider upgrading or replacing their handguns very low on their list of priorities. If the gun works acceptably well, it tends to stay in service for a loooong time, especially in large armies where the cost of testing and reequipping with new weapons would be immense.

Most truly serious combat handgun aficionados are, I'm sure, aware that in "The Pistol in War" chapter from Herbert W. McBride's book *A Rifleman Went to War*, the author is very complimentary toward the 1911/.45 ACP's performance as a wartime combat weapon. I've been aware of McBride's handgun anecdotes for years, and frankly I've never been impressed. If you ever get the chance, dear readers, you should take a gander at some of the "war stories" to come out of Europe. Did you know that Europeans commonly consider the 9mm Parabellum an awesome combat pistol cartridge and the .45 ACP incredibly overrated, exactly the opposite of the traditional American opinion? I think there's probably a certain amount of self-regulation going on here. In a real war, if you're down to firing a handgun in defense of your skin, then things are grim. When an American soldier shot someone with his .45 and it actually worked, he felt so lucky to be alive in the aftermath that he couldn't stop babbling to anyone who'd listen about how instantly effective the cartridge was. And in all the cases where someone up against a wall shot an opponent with his trusty .45 and it *didn't* work . . . well, that person wasn't subsequently available to go around telling people, "You know, that .45 didn't work worth a damn," because he was a little too busy being DEAD! And that same phenomenon is why Europeans are so high on the Nine.

Really, handguns *are* almost useless in modern warfare. This reminds me of an incident recounted in a book written by a Marine lieutenant about his experiences in Vietnam. It seems he and another LT were dug in tight in their position one night, and they kept getting strafed by AK fire . . . and I mean constantly! In his book the author said something to the effect of, "This one guy with an AK kept firing at us for hours." (Now, if it was me in his position, I probably would've figured it wasn't one guy with 100 magazines firing me up, but rather a whole bunch of people *all* armed with AKs . . . but what do I know?) So, after this constant ak-ak-ak goes on seemingly forever, the other lieutenant stands up, pulls out his .45, and says, "I've had it with this shit; I'm going out there to get that guy!" to which the author replies, "Sit the fuck down. You're going out there with *that?* Rifles are for fighting; handguns are for jerking off." * Now, I don't think I'd go that far, but I have to admit this guy had a point: I mean, would *you* want to be armed with a handgun in the middle of a real war when everyone else had rifles? I think not.

I don't mean to discount out of hand the 1911's record of military service, for it certainly exists, and there were indeed soldiers over the years who did some impressive things with the big auto. The definitive 1911 military exploit was, of course, York's. Lt. Sam Woodfill used a .45 auto to good effect while wiping out a series of German machine gun emplacements in the Meuse-Argonne Campaign of

---

* That rather hurt our poor would-be handgun hero's feelings, apparently, but it also probably saved his life: he sat back down.

World War I in the fall of 1918, an action for which he won the Medal of Honor. Marine Sgt. Herbert Henry Hanneken used a 1911 to terminate Haitian insurgent leader Charlemagne Peralte with a single well-placed round of .45 hardball (a feat that certainly did the reputation of .45 ball no harm); this was the culmination of a brilliant and daring plan for which Hanneken was also awarded the Medal of Honor. A host of lesser-known heroes have also used the "Army .45" well. However, I feel this had less to do with the gun itself and more to do with the quality of the men wielding it. Americans have a tendency to deify technology, to be very impressed with gadgetry and ignore the human element. What we don't realize is that when a pistol stays service standard for three-quarters of a century as did the 1911, in so large a fighting force as the U.S. military, the law of averages makes it absolutely inevitable that every so often a truly extraordinary soldier is going to come along to do wonderful things with the issue sidearm no matter what it is. Personally, I'm waiting for the first time an American soldier is presented the Medal of Honor for using a Beretta 92 in battle. Now that'll put a crimp in some .45 fans' underwear!

"The ruggedness and reliability of the 1911 auto are unsurpassed."

Nope. The 1911 auto is in many ways a fairly fragile handgun, and small parts breakage is common. The most delicate areas include the plunger tube (prone to snapping off), the barrel bushing (which can fracture), and the extractor (prone to losing its tension, resulting in failures to extract or fully eject). I have had all of these things occur to me in new guns of top quality, featuring either the stock factory parts or primo aftermarket equivalents. Shooters of my acquaintance tell me that, on their 1911s that are shot extensively, the slide stop has a tendency to break where the swinging link rides it. The swinging link itself is, according to pistolsmiths with whom I've discussed the matter, prone to breakage as well. I've never personally seen these last two events occur, but I do believe what those people have told me. I *have* watched another man shoot a 1911 with his thumb riding the safety lever in the "Gunsite technique" when the safety lever snapped off. (Cut the *hell* out of his hand, by the way.) This was with the factory thumb safety, not an aftermarket unit, and his gun was of good marque, not some El Cheapo knockoff.

Reliability-wise, the 1911 takes a backseat to many of the more modern auto pistols. The 1911 was designed to feed hardball, and no matter what you do to it, there's really no way around that fact. Now, I'm not one of those folks who says you should only carry hardball in a 1911, but I do say that the further your hollowpoint departs from a rounded, hardball-like ogive, the more you're asking for trouble with this gun. Feed a 1911 a bullet shape it doesn't like and it will malfunction with obstinate frequency.

"What else can you name that's 85 years old and many experts still consider to be state-of-the-art?"

I think this has a lot do with deep-dyed conservatism and a fear of the future among many firearms enthusiasts. Shooters in general seem to be a pretty tradition-minded, hidebound lot. Think about it: every major change or advance in the field of the handgun, when it appeared, was opposed by many "experts." Thus, the ideas of the self-contained cartridge, smokeless powder, the double-action (DA) revolver, semiautomatic pistols, aluminum-framed handguns, stainless steel as a gun material, holding the gun in two hands and/or using the sights for combat shooting, polymer frames, the 9mm Parabellum cartridge, DA autos, etc., were all decried as the next thing to heresy. Boy, if those folks had had their way, we'd still be firing cap-and-ball revolvers (point shooting, of course)!

"A single-action auto like the 1911 is the easiest gun to learn to shoot really well. Its short, light, consistent trigger pull makes it so simple you can learn to fire the gun in just 10 minutes."

While the actual process of firing a single-action (SA) auto is easier than that of any other type of serious defensive handgun, there is more to carrying and shooting a SA auto than simply hitting the trigger. You must also incorporate disengagement of the cocked and locked SA auto's thumb safety into a reflexive part of the draw stroke.

Exercise physiologists say it takes between 3,000 and 5,000 correct repetitions of a movement before it becomes an unconscious reaction. If you can accomplish that in 10 minutes, let me know! I shall wait for you here.

"I want to carry a Colt .45 (because, of course, it's the ultimate handgun), but I'm just not comfortable carrying a gun with a cocked hammer. If I carry the gun hammer-down, is there any way I can get it into action fast with only one hand?"

When they find themselves in a real fight, many times even those shooters trained exclusively in two-handed fire wind up loosing at least their first few shots one-handed. There can be any number of reasons for this: the most commonly touted explanation, of course, is that one arm is disabled. Having to use one hand to fend off a close-range assailant, or hold a flashlight, operate a light switch, open a door, drag another person to safety, etc., while the strong hand goes for the gun can also create a situation where you *must* be able to bring your defensive equipment into play one-handed.

Frankly, after talking to folks who've audited a hell of a lot more gunfights than I have, I believe the most common reason the defender's opening shots are often fired with one hand is that, in contrast to most range simulations where the shooter starts out facing the target, in the real world the attacker often comes in from the side or rear, and turning swiftly to engage the enemy causes the off-hand to automatically extend itself away from the body for balance.

It is generally accepted that there are three safe states in which the 1911 auto may be carried. In the system popularized by Jeff Cooper, these are referred to as Conditions One, Two, and Three. Condition One (aka "cocked and locked") consists of carrying the gun with the hammer back on a round in the chamber, thumb safety applied; Condition Two has the hammer down on a chambered cartridge; and Condition Three means hammer down on an empty chamber. (In all three of these states it is assumed a full magazine has been inserted into the gun.)

If the single action auto is carried in any manner other than cocked and locked, it is considerably slower and more fumble-prone when it is brought into action than either DA revolvers or other types of autos—and that's even if you've got both hands available. Get down to one-handed manipulation and it's no contest. Unfortunately for the fellow who wanted to tote his 1911 hammer-down and bring it into action one-handed, Condition One is the only carry mode in which the gun can be drawn and fired swiftly and smoothly with one hand. Condition Two requires cocking the hammer during the draw and is terribly slow and uncertain. Condition Three pretty much requires two hands to cycle a round into the chamber. Over the years, there have been people who've worked on things like racking the slide of a chamber-empty 1911 on the holster as the gun is drawn; however, in my opinion, this comes under the heading of "dangerous stunt," not something on which you'd want to bet your life.

Now, disengaging the safety on a Condition One SA auto *off-hand* only can be a bit challenging unless the gun's been fitted with ambidextrous safety levers. But (assuming good training), readying the cocked-and-locked auto to fire with the off-hand only is *still* easier than strong-hand-only manipulation of the same gun from Condition Two or Three.

For those of you who want to carry an auto but are uncomfortable carrying a SA cocked and locked, we have a solution for you: it's called the DA auto pistol! Or how about carrying a revolver? (These days it's hard to make a case for the revolver as a first-choice combat handgun [see Chapter 6], but there's no doubt it's a superior choice to a hammer-down SA auto.) How 'bout a DA-*only* auto? Whichever way you decide to go, I *strongly* suggest that you not carry your defense gun in such a fashion that it absolutely requires two hands to put it into use. If you ever do need the gun, it's likely that you might not *have* two hands available!

"A .45 auto's *gotta* be harder to shoot than a 9mm. Just look at the greater amount of recoil."

The more I learn about shooting, the more I realize that, within reason, recoil has almost nothing to do with how quickly and accurately a gun can be fired. Having good shooting technique matters.

The type of trigger action the gun possesses matters tremendously. How the gun fits your hand matters. Recoil? Doesn't matter. With good technique, either a 9mm or .45 will be back down from recoil before most people could hit the trigger again, anyway.

"All the studies (Thompson-LaGarde, Marshall, Ayoob, Strasbourg) agree that in full-metal jacket form the .45 ACP beats the smaller bores." [From a letter I received recently.]

That's debatable. The Thompson-LaGarde tests have been pretty well discredited for years. In Evan Marshall's findings, the difference in performance between 9mm and .45 ball is so minuscule it can be easily explained away as a statistical fluctuation. Since Ayoob never reveals the details of his findings, it's impossible to critique his data. Finally, in the Strasbourg tests the Average Incapacitation Time for 9mm ball versus .45 ball was 14.4 seconds versus 13.84 seconds, respectively, for a grand total difference in performance of .56 second. Whippee.

Going on about full-metal jacket performance, my correspondent commented, "This is *not* academic in New Jersey, Canada, or the armed forces." Conversely, if you're not in New Jersey, Canada, or the armed forces (and most of us are that fortunate), it is academic.

There is a whole raft of myths regarding .45 hardball, none of which are supported by fact. How about this one:

"It seems we have to keep relearning the same lessons, generation after generation. These days, there seems to be a fascination with the medium-bore calibers. How tragic that we didn't learn from the experiences of our forebears, early in this century, when their .38-caliber revolvers were found wanting against the Philippine Moros, and the U.S. Army was forced to develop the mighty, manstopping .45 auto to solve the problem."

It is true that the 1911 auto was developed at least partially in response to the failure of the .38 Long Colt revolver to stop the tough, fanatical Moro warriors. This led to the caliber of the military sidearm being changed to .45, first in the .45 Colt revolver Model 1909, then to .45 ACP in the semiauto Model of 1911. Where the myth starts is in the idea that the .45 proved any more effective than the .38. According to historical records, the Moros were equally unimpressed by a hardball-loaded .45 auto. Actually, the .30-40 Krag rifle was far from a dependable "stopper" against these determined warriors. The only portable firearm with a good record for "Moro-stopping" was a buckshot-loaded Winchester Model 1897 12-gauge shotgun!

"Yeah, you're pretty good with that little popgun. Of course, it all changes when you move up to a .45!" [Heard from shooters explaining to you why you were able to outshoot them and their highly customized SA .45s using a stock DA 9mm.]

Moving right along, there is still an immense amount of controversy among gun-knowledgeable .45 men over Colt's mid-1980s incorporation of its excellent automatic firing pin lock into the 1911 auto. There are two statements in particular relating to this part that I feel should be addressed:

(1) "Even Colt admitted how unsafe their design was, and that it would discharge if you dropped the gun, by adding the firing pin lock." (2) "I don't like the firing pin lock: it simply clutters up the design, and besides, I don't trust it to move out of the way and let the gun fire in a defensive emergency."

Let's discuss this a bit. I must be the only person in the world who can take or leave the 1911 firing pin lock. When my 1911 has this part, I can live with it and I don't worry about it. Similarly, when it doesn't have a firing pin lock, I can live with it and I don't worry about it. There have indeed been cases over the years where 1911s have fired when dropped on the muzzle, and I'm aware of at least one man who was seriously shot up when the firing pin lock on his stainless steel Colt Officer's ACP seized up at "the moment of truth." However, there's one fact that most people seem to forget when obsessing about such possibilities: neither of these things is going to happen to a gun in good mechanical condition!

In the 1970s, the old firm of Detonics conducted tests to see just how much impact was required to make a cocked-and-locked 1911 fire when it hit the ground. They rigged up a system of strings to guide the gun so it would always land on the muzzle and started dropping it from ever-increasing heights. They found it was necessary to drop the gun from the equivalent of a three-story building and have the piece land directly on its muzzle to occasion an inertial discharge. If that is the case (and I assure you it is), then why have certain 1911s over the years discharged when dropped from belt level during the draw? Why, I'm glad you asked! Remember, the 1911 has been with us for eight and a half decades now. Many of those old guns are beat to hell. I remember when I was in the Army, cleaning several old .45s where the firing pin springs had become so compressed over the decades, they were much shorter than they should have been . . . well, it wouldn't surprise me if one of those pieces lit off when dropped! However, that simply does-n't happen with guns featuring new, full-power firing pin springs. I like the extra power firing pin springs, like those provided by Wolff Gunsprings free of charge with every aftermarket recoil spring it sells; every time I change my recoil spring, I replace this part as well. Even though I understand intellectually that the factory firing pin spring is perfectly safe, I have to admit that for me one of these extra power parts takes a lot of the worry out of being close.

Many people who are unfamiliar with the 1911 seem to fear that the cocked gun is suddenly going to fire itself in the holster. In fact, *Handguns* magazine once ran an article penned by one worthy who actually had this happen to him. (And all over the country, people who've distrusted the cocked-and-locked 1911 for years screamed, "I KNEW IT!") Again, the cause can be traced to an old gun that was not in safe mechanical condition. Without being nasty here, I do have to ask one question about this fellow's experience: if he were really the gun expert his article shows he obviously believes himself to be, then why didn't he know how to perform a simple armorer's check on his 1911, which would have instantly shown that his hammer/sear engagement was not within safe limits? Why wasn't he smart

enough to even attempt this? I mean, I do this with every 1911 I eval-
uate (or carry), even if it's a brand-new, out-of-the-box gun, much
less the well over half-century old piece he was toting!

Now, to the people who distrust the firing pin lock: I'm only aware
of one occasion where a good guy ever got ventilated because this part
malfunctioned. A very accomplished shooter found himself facing
three armed opponents. He pulled his stainless Officer's ACP .45, and
the gun refused to fire! Sounds like a nightmare, doesn't it? Luckily,
after an extended hospital stay, he survived the encounter. Now, that's
enough to sour you on firing pin locks for life; however, the cause of
the failure did not lie with this part, but rather was the result of incompetent customization. Basically, our hero paid a hack pistolsmith good
money to turn a reliable handgun into one that nearly got him killed.
Just as 1911s in good operating condition don't go off when you drop
them, or fire themselves in their holsters, 1911s with firing pin locks
don't malfunction either—unless something is seriously wrong!

"The most delicate parts in a Colt are the Series 80 parts."

Untrue. In actuality these parts are overengineered and massive
for the job they're asked to do. The most fragile part in a 1911 is the
plunger tube that runs between the slide stop and thumb safety. This
tube contains two small plungers and a spring, the power of which
serves both to prevent the slide stop from popping up into the slide-
stop notch under recoil until pushed into engagement by an empty
magazine's follower, and to hold the thumb safety in the "safe" or
"fire" position. (The plunger tube is actually one of the most complicated and expensive parts of the 1911 to machine.)

In the classic 1911 design, the plunger tube is affixed to the gun
only by two small studs that pass into the frame. On the end of each
stud is machined a small cup. When the plunger tube is installed in the
gun a special staking tool is used to swage and expand the thin sides
of the hollowed-out stud ends, providing a press fit in the holes
through the frame. Unfortunately, every time you flip your thumb
safety on or off, stress is placed upon that part, and it is not at all
unusual for the rearward of those two studs, the one closest to the

thumb safety, to snap off. When that happens, the thumb safety winds up in an intermediate position, halfway between "on" and "off safe."

I've had this happen to me while firing the totally stock Colt Government Model that was my carry gun for a year in the early 1990s. I've also watched another shooter fire his near-stock Springfield Government Model at a handgun training class when the exact same thing happened to him. A good friend of mine had the plunger tube on his Delta Elite come loose during the gun's very first shooting session. My friend and fellow gunwriter Tom Graham tells me he saw many instances of this breakage on Army issue .45s during his days as a military armorer.

All this is troubling, but at one time I would have said it wasn't really that big a deal, since in an emergency it would be possible to physically hold the thumb safety down and still fire the piece. Then, at a training class I attended, a female shooter's 1911 had the plunger tube, not snap off, but pull out slightly from the frame. When that happened, the plunger popped out underneath the tab on the thumb safety lever, blocking downward movement of this part, and it was impossible to flip the thumb safety from the "safe" to "fire" position. Now *that's* frightening!

In the mid-1990s Colt began countersinking the holes in the frame through which the plunger tube's studs fit. This makes it possible to expand the ends of those studs far more than had previously been the case, so that now they actually flow up and over the holes through which they are inserted. I am told by top-flight pistolsmiths that this upgrade has almost done away with the problems of plunger tubes snapping off or pulling out of frames. Still, call me conservative, but having seen so many serious failures in this area I find cold comfort in "almost."

One thing I like very much about the Para-Ordnance guns is that the plunger tube is an integral part of the frame, so there's no way for it to snap off or come loose, tying up the gun. If only these high-cap 1911s weren't so big and heavy that they'd make great boat anchors, we'd be set! I think a good rule of thumb for a gun that is to be carried constantly concealed is that it not weigh more than 35 ounces fully loaded. (Now, my constantly concealed carry guns for years were Colt Government Models and Combat Commanders—approximately 44 ounces and 42 ounces loaded, respectively—so it can be done, but it's a bit of a pain.) Even the "compact" Para-Ordnance P12 with an aluminum alloy frame doesn't make our weight limit, and my Cylinder & Slide Shop custom Para (done up on a full-sized steel-framed P14), according to ye olde postal scale, weighs exactly 52.4 ounces loaded. Wow!

And now, one of my personal favorites:

"The .45 has got to be better than the 9mm. After all, you don't *really* think Sergeant York could have stopped that German bayonet charge with a 9mm, do you?"

Well, actually . . . yes, I do! While Sgt. (then Cpl.) Alvin York's incredible feat of dropping six charging men with his Colt Government Model is the stuff of legends, it is not the most devastating use of a handgun in modern combat. That honor must go to 2d Lt. Lourens Marthinus Janse van Vuuren, the South African soldier who, in 1975 in a bloody battle in Angola, killed 11 Cuban soldiers with his Star Model BS 9mm. When I was discussing this incident with fellow gunwriter Leroy Thompson, he commented, "I guess you could argue that van Vuuren couldn't have done that with a .45 . . . because he wouldn't have been carrying enough ammo!" Actually, I rather doubt that, since the single-column eight-round magazine in the Model BS doesn't give you much more ammo than the seven-round mags found in military-issue 1911s . . . but it makes a great quote! With nine rounds of 9mm in the gun and one spare magazine, van Vuuren killed 11 enemy soldiers with 17 cartridges. His first nine shots were fired weak-handed; the index finger of van Vuuren's right hand had been crushed just prior to the gunfight. He only scored four kills for nine rounds fired thus. After that, he reloaded and by then was pumping enough adrenalin that he simply didn't *care* his trigger finger was crushed. With his dominant right hand, crushed trigger finger and all, he scored seven kills for eight rounds of 9mm, performance even a sharpshooter like Sergeant York would've approved of!

Just as Alvin York received the Medal of Honor for his actions in the Argonne Forest of France in 1918, Lourens van Vuuren was awarded the Honoris Crux (Cross of Honor), South Africa's highest award for heroism in combat. It is interesting to note that York's sidearm was the John Browning-designed Model of 1911 and van Vuuren's Model BS was simply a slightly modified 1911 chambered for 9mm. How strange to think of these two men, these two soldiers from different countries in different wars, separated from each other by almost six decades and a world of distance, both beset by overwhelming odds, both defending themselves, successfully, with guns not all that much different from each other!

After the foregoing statement appeared in an article in a national gun magazine, I received a letter stating in part, "The story of van Vuuren is indeed interesting, but you forgot a few key facts. Correct me if I'm wrong but: (1) van Vuuren was in a tank or APC [armored personnel carrier] at the time, so the Cubans couldn't shoot him with small arms; (2) because he was behind armor, an instant stop wasn't necessary as it was in York's case; (3) the Cubans were stoned on marijuana; (4) the 11 Cuban soldiers didn't charge as a group; rather, they happened by a few at a time; (5) some, if not most, of the Cubans didn't know they had a problem until van Vuuren fired. You didn't tell the complete story, only the parts that made the 9mm look good. Van Vuuren did some great shooting and deserved the medal, but he didn't stop 11 charging Cubans while he was in immediate danger of being overrun as you suggested in the story. Like the 1911 pistol, van Vuuren's incredible story can stand on its own without you creating a colossal handgun myth around it."

It amazes me that this guy could actually make the statement "van Vuuren's story can stand on its own" when everything else he says makes it abundantly clear he knows next to nothing about it! Oh well, he did say "correct me if I'm wrong" . . . so I guess I'll just go ahead and correct him.

The statements, "the Cubans were stoned on marijuana," "happened by a few at a time," and "some, if not most, of the Cubans didn't know they had a problem until van Vuuren fired," are purest bullshit (this is, unfortunately, the sort of thing we hear all too commonly from 1911 auto/.45 ACP fans attempting to denigrate any other gun/caliber besides their pet). The only thing he was indisputably right about was the fact that van Vuuren was firing from inside an armored car (an Eland 90, to be precise). I almost sent him a copy of Jack Lott's 1990 article on the van Vuuren firefight so he could actually know what he was talking about the next time he discussed these events, but then I said to myself, "Naaaaah!"

(It's highly debatable, by the way, whether York's stops were "instant." York stated that every one of the six men he nailed with his .45 thrashed around and "screamed just like pigs" for awhile after he shot them.)

I must say, I did resent the implication that I deliberately "didn't tell the complete story, only the parts that made the 9mm look good." Quite aside from the slur on my character, I assure you, faithful readers, that the 9mm-versus-.45 debate, which has occupied feeble minds for generations, holds no interest for me. What a worthless dispute! The only thing you'll ever hear *me* talking about while addressing this time-worn foolishness would be, as in this chapter, to point out just how stupid the entire "controversy" is and how senseless are the arguments put forth by those attempting to reinforce their positions in this matter. And even that bores me.

However, I certainly didn't intend to give the impression by my comments that van Vuuren had "stopped 11 charging Cubans while he was in immediate danger of being overrun," so perhaps it might not be untoward here to take a more in-depth look at van Vuuren's exploits than was possible or appropriate in my magazine article. The information I'm about to recount to you comes from Lott's excellent and previously mentioned piece on this affair.

In 1975, the 21-year-old Second Lieutenant van Vuuren was sent to Angola as the commander of a troop of four armored cars to participate in the "Savannah" campaign as a member of "Foxbat Force" (the code name for a clandestine mobile force in which the Eland 90 played a crucial role as a fighting reconnaissance vehicle). Actually, on the day of van Vuuren's famous firefight, his troop consisted of only three Elands, since one of the machines had electrical problems even before the mission began. During heavy fighting deep inside

Angola, van Vuuren's Eland 90, stalled with near-dead batteries and with its tires shot out, was surrounded by approximately 20 Cuban soldiers who rained AK fire on the disabled vehicle. His Eland was down to only one shell for its main gun (which was in any event useless against the troops, who were literally swarming over it), and the other two cars in van Vuuren's troop had backed off and were unable to provide fire support because they were totally out of ammunition. Foot soldiers armed with rifles and grenades had little to fear from an immobilized armored car incapable of firing on them, so the Cubans closed in for the kill. In situations such as this, the supposedly "protective" armored car becomes instead a vulnerable steel cell.

Two Cubans jumped on van Vuuren's Eland from behind. Another armored car commander in van Vuuren's troop brought his vehicle in to 100 meters and shot them off with his 7.62 x 51mm FAL rifle. With death staring him in the face (and that's not just a figure of speech—Cuban soldiers were so close he could see the beads of sweat on their features), van Vuuren considered having a go at the enemy with the spanners (heavy wrenches) in his armored car, but then remembered his service pistol. He drew his Star Model BS 9mm, but the pain from his crushed finger was so intense (the index finger on van Vuuren's right hand had been badly mashed by the breech block of his car's 90mm gun in recoil shortly before the festivities *really* began to heat up) that he switched it over to his left hand, threw open the pistol port on the Eland's left side (designed for just such emergencies), and opened fire, killing four Cubans before his slide locked back.

The Cubans ignored their dead and pressed the attack. Several were trying to pry open the armored car's hatch (for obvious reasons). At this moment a hideous if apt memory jolted through van Vuuren. He had seen "armored" scarab beetles overwhelmed and killed by a swarm of ants. In the urgency of the situation the pain of his crushed trigger finger was forgotten; van Vuuren switched the Star to his right hand and reloaded with his only spare eight-round magazine. By the time the gun was again empty, seven more Cubans lay dead.

The injured Eland took off, flat tires and all, running down two Cubans with AKs in the process. Lieutenant van Vuuren and his battered troop of Elands limped back to field headquarters, where his fingernail was removed and the finger stitched up. Later, South African soldiers, including van Vuuren, returned to the site of the battle to tally the dead, and marijuana was found in some of the Cuban's pockets—hardly surprising in a land where the plant is commonly grown and used by natives. (So now we know where the idea that all the Cubans were stoned on marijuana, however patently ridiculous, came from.)

Now, having addressed all that, we must indeed acknowledge that in any comparison of "Coolest Under Fire" or "Faced the Greatest Danger" the nod must surely go to Alvin York over Lourens van Vuuren. Since van Vuuren was firing through the pistol port of his armored car while York faced the German bayonet charge under conditions of equal combat, it can certainly be argued that York's feat was more impressive than van Vuuren's. (As a matter of fact, Alvin York is one of my personal heroes. See Chapter 4 on York in this book.) However, that sort of comparison is not what I was doing in my original article; rather, I was comparing the performance of the two men and the respective handgun cartridges they used in the category of casualties inflicted. In that respect, we must go with van Vuuren, as I said, "the most devastating use of a handgun in modern combat," i.e., "the most enemy soldiers killed with a handgun by a single soldier in a single engagement."

SUMMARY

By now you've probably come to the conclusion that I hate the 1911, right? Nothing could be further from the truth. I chose Colt Government Models and Combat Commanders as my constant concealed-carry guns for years, and during that time I developed a deep and abiding love for those hefty handguns and their big ol' bullet. What I *can't* stand are those people who attempt to justify their preference for this gun/cartridge combination by relying on unsubstantiated myths, "war stories," and emotional rhetoric.

For whatever reason, the 1911 .45 auto cult tends to attract more than its fair share of sloped foreheads and bully-boy types who approach their devotion to this gun and caliber with pseudo-religious fervor. There are some sad cases out there whose entire identities are tied into the guns they carry: the 1911 is their religion, the .45 their God, and I'm absolutely certain that nothing I've said in this chapter is going to have the slightest effect on them. It is by definition impossible to reason with an unreasonable person, and many 1911/.45 auto aficionados are running on pure emotion. Because they're not thinking logically, logic will not penetrate their thought processes. You can stand in front of one of these guys and point out that many of the arguments commonly put forth in favor of the 1911 auto and .45 ACP cartridge are myths, then back up that statement with facts, and it's like your words hit a concrete wall around his cranium—THUNK!

Nor do I have much sympathy for those folks who attempt to bolster their own beliefs by running down every other type of handgun, or handgun caliber, out there. The amount of venom some .45 fans have toward the 9mm Parabellum cartridge in particular approaches the absurd . . . actually, I take that back, it *is* absurd! These people just can't stand it that the 9mm is far more popular among serious self-defense-oriented shooters, federal agencies, and police departments than their baby. (If the .45 ACP is God, then the 9mm is The Adversary. Imagine how a born-again Christian would feel surrounded and outnumbered by Satanists.) Of course, .45 fans are quick to point out that the *real* reason so many benighted souls prefer the 9mm, or any other inferior choice, is because "most people can't handle the power of the .45." Uh, yeah, right. For some people the statement, "To each his own," translates into, "Everyone must agree with me, and if they don't they're fools."

Read the ridiculous myths I've addressed in this chapter and then go out and fire a Colt .45 auto. Great gun, huh? There is an entire complex mythology surrounding this gun design and its primary chambering, but when the myths are stripped away, what's left is this simple reality: the 1911 .45 auto *is* a great handgun, and in the harsh light of truth it can stand on its own very real merits!

CHAPTER TWO

DOUBLE-ACTION AUTOS

Always listen to experts. They'll tell you what can't be done, and why. Then do it.

—Lazarus Long
in *Time Enough for Love*
by Robert A. Heinlein

It is a commonplace of gunwriting, especially among devotees of the SA auto pistol, to bemoan the difficulty of firing a DA auto well, especially under the stress of a defensive emergency. We are told (a) that these weapons' long, heavy initial trigger pull makes a fast first shot all but impossible, (b) that the transition to the short, light trigger pull for the second shot will result in your first two rounds impacting to different points of aim, (c) that the two types of trigger pulls require different trigger finger placements, and (d) that switching between these two finger positions will screw up your rhythm so badly that any sort of speed and accuracy between your first two shots is unattainable (the so-called "crunch-tick" syndrome).

I find all these statements to be false *if* a shooter is armed with a DA auto featuring decent trigger pulls *and* if the gun fits his hand. For two years my carry gun was a 9mm SIG P228. I used to absolutely love taking that gun to pistol matches and handgun training classes and kicking ass on most, if not all, of the folks armed with expensive, highly customized SA autos. (It *can* be done, folks!)

I remember one match I attended where I came in second place (by about one percentage point) right behind fellow shooter Rich Bitow. Now, Rich is a fine pistol shot in his own right, and he likes running highly customized 1911s. I was firing against him with my stock P228. After the match, Rich said to me, "I'm really impressed you could come that close to tying me with a double-action auto."

I replied, "Well, thanks for the compliment, but, really, my attitude is that if I chose this gun to shoot against you, I should be able to beat you with this gun. I'm not making any excuses. You just shot better than I did." (After all, a good craftsman doesn't blame his tools, and I have zero sympathy for people who whine after losing, "Well, things would've been different if my gun were easier to shoot.")

Rich laughed and said, "Weeeeell, I do think my custom 1911's trigger pull gave me a *bit* of an advantage over you."

I said, "Well, again, thanks for the compliment. Just out of curiosity, what *is* the trigger pull on your gun?"

"Oh, a pound and a half."

"Uh, yeah," I gulped, "you might've had a slight advantage there!"

You'll often hear the statement that today's competition speed shooters favor SA autos because having a short, light trigger pull for every shot is the system that allows them the absolute maximum in marksmanship performance. And I do not question that. What I do question is the idea that DA autos are innately much inferior to their SA brethren in potential performance. You know, these days we have stock gun matches, revolver-only matches, Glock-only matches, 1911-only matches . . . what I'd really like to see, on the national level, would be a "DA autos only" International Practical Shooting Confederation (IPSC) competition. Of course, it'll never happen, but wouldn't it be interesting to see just how long that old chestnut about the impossibility of firing DA autos fast and well lasts once you start paying the best shooters in the world to push these guns to the limit? This is just my personal take on it, but I feel there probably would be a minor drop in performance, compared to the same shooters using their highly tricked-out 1911s, but I'll bet the difference would be a lot smaller than many people would suppose.

I try to be careful, myself, of making blanket statements, and it really sets my teeth on edge to read or hear something like, "SA autos are the best combat weapons because they can be so easily fired. DA autos are simply impossible to handle well in a real stress situation. If you're armed with a double-action auto in a real gunfight, you've got a choice: either slow way down and grind your way through that horrendous DA trigger pull, or throw the first shot into the dirt to get the gun to the controllable SA state." There are actually people pro-pounding this drivel as a realistic response to a close-range, life-or-death defensive emergency! These folks honestly believe the SA auto is so greatly superior to its DA equivalent that a shooter armed with the latter is suffering under an insurmountable disadvantage. (Such ardent SA devotees live in a black-and-white world, when in reality the world is composed of infinite shades of gray.) Well, it ain't nec-essarily so, guys! Personally, I find that many SA auto fanciers are mediocre shots, so dependent on their SA crutches they are barely competent with their chosen firearm and useless with anything more demanding. A skilled pistolero armed with a DA auto can annihilate the average shooter armed with a SA auto!

When I was attending Massad Ayoob's LFI-2 course at his train-ing school, the Lethal Force Institute, one of the drills that students had to execute entailed drawing from the holster and hitting a four-inch circle at seven yards. Easy enough, you say? Well, what made this drill fun was that everyone in the class competed against every-one else at once, in an eliminations fashion, until only one shooter was left! We started with the entire class (about 40 shooters) on line, and at the signal we all drew and fired. Everyone whose shot hit out-side their circle had to step back off the line. We did that a few times until the line had been winnowed down so much, there were few enough of us still up there, that the instructors could tell which shooter got off his shot *last* after drawing and firing. The last shoot-er to fire on each run then had to step down. This turned up the pres-sure, because not only did you have to be accurate enough to hit your target, but you had to be fast enough to ensure you weren't the last person to fire.

In short order, the line had melted down to three people: myself with my DA SIG, one guy armed with a "Safe Action" Glock 17L longslide (in essence a SA gun), and another with a cocked and locked SA Government Model .45 auto. And there we stayed for quite a while. All three of us just refused to miss, and we were getting off our shots so close together the instructors couldn't pick out one of us as being last. It sounded like this: "Shooters ready? Stand by . . ." Whissstle! BOOM! Three shots sounded as one. "Anybody miss? No? Well, I couldn't tell who was last . . . let's do it again!" Finally, I pulled a shot outside my target circle. If memory serves me correctly, it was the guy with the Government Model who finally won the whole shebang. But the point is, my DA auto and I proved perfectly capable of performing at the same level as two other very experienced shooters, both of whom were armed with extremely user-friendly, short-trigger-pull handguns.

After I finally came off the line, several people said to me, "Damn, I can't believe you were shooting a double-action auto so well you could keep up with a Glock and a Government Model! How did you *do* that?" I thought about it for a moment.

"Well, it probably has something to do with the fact that I've carried this gun almost every day for the past two years; in that time I've put over 5,000 rounds through it, and I'd be scared to guess how many tens of thousands of times I've dry-fired it!" Even at a reasonably high level of competition, you don't have to feel like a red-headed stepchild if you're shooting a DA auto. If you're well practiced and skilled with the technology, you can step right up and play with the big boys.

The DA auto's heavy, long first trigger pull is the reason most armchair gunfighters dislike this weapon. It's also the reason many police departments love it. Indeed, most police agencies forbid SA autos as duty weapons for line officers. Frankly, those police administrators have got a point. The average cop falls into the category of being a semi-trained, nondedicated shooter who has absolutely no business carrying a SA auto out in the real world. These guns' ultra-short and light trigger pulls make them entirely too prone to accidental discharge, especially under stress, to be issued across the board as police duty weapons. (The well-trained, dedicated officer can, of course, be safe carrying any weapon he prefers, including a SA auto.)

Really, when you think about it, the DA auto trigger system makes an incredible amount of sense. Most cops and civilians will never be in a gunfight. They will, however, handle their guns hundreds or even thousands of times, with all the possibilities for accidental discharge that entails. The weight and length of the DA auto's trigger pull can provide an important safety margin when a handgun is being manipulated by less-than-expert hands (i.e., most people). Some idealists will say, "That's a matter of training, not a matter of gun design, and people who don't know enough to keep their finger off the trigger have no business carrying handguns. Keep your index finger out of the trigger guard and a SA auto is perfectly safe." Now, that is undoubtedly true, and it's a nice ideal. However, in the real world, people with less-than-expert skill levels often do wind up carrying and using handguns, and to base your attitude toward firearms safety on the way you think the world *should* be, instead of the way the world *is*, strikes me as more than a little stupid.

Most times when a cop or civilian points a gun at a bad guy, he doesn't wind up needing to actually shoot the person. The threat of being shot is usually sufficient to send the felon running away or cow him into compliance. It is extremely important, therefore, that you not accidentally shoot a cooperative or fleeing opponent. Having a DA first shot in your gun, with double-digit poundage to the trigger pull that requires most of an inch of trigger travel before the gun fires, can be an important hedge against accidental discharge under stress. Yes, yes, a thousand times yes, I agree that training is more important than the particulars of the gun design with which you are armed. And, yes, it is true that keeping your finger outside the trigger guard unless you're actually firing or about to fire the piece is a mandatory habit for the well-trained shooter. However, again, in the real world, the majority of people carrying and using guns are not well-trained (although it would surely be nice if they were). When most people feel threatened by a criminal, so much so they wind up pointing a gun at their potential robber, mugger, rapist, or murderer, trigger fingers do have a tendency to gravitate toward triggers.

Pretending that is not the case and simply sniffing, "Good training would prevent that," constitutes wishful thinking and a refusal to accept reality that is almost criminal in its severity.

Now, if a DA first shot is such a desirable handgun feature for most people, how about the gun switching to the short, light SA trigger pull for every shot thereafter? Why, I'm glad you asked! With far shorter and lighter trigger pulls, the gun becomes considerably easier to shoot fast and well, with a concomitantly higher hit potential under stress. The best summary of the virtues of the DA auto I've ever heard came from firearms instructor Greg Hamilton: "Most of the time when you point a gun at someone, you won't need to shoot, so you want it to be necessary that you make a conscious decision, that you exercise a deliberate effort, to fire that first shot. But when you've already fired that first shot . . . that probably means you're in a fight, so what you want then is a gun that's easy to shoot!" And that's what the DA auto gives you: a sidearm that's hard to fire accidentally for the first shot, but once you're in a fight it instantly metamorphoses into a gun that's extremely easy to shoot fast and well.

I have to say, I wonder if one of the big reasons many people seem to have such problems firing DA autos well is simply because they've been told they should. For decades, it has been a cliché of firearms instruction for teachers routinely to tell their students, "Yep, the DA auto is the hardest type of handgun to shoot really well. The long, first-shot trigger stroke gives shooters problems; transitioning to the short trigger pull for succeeding shots is a pain; the first two shots tend to impact to entirely different points." And then those shooters get out there, try these guns for the first time, and lo and behold!, they have problems with the first long trigger stroke, transitioning to the shorter trigger pulls for succeeding shots, and keeping their first two shots together . . . imagine that! Never underestimate the power of suggestion.

I think a lot of the blame (or credit, depending on your point of view) for this state of affairs can be laid at the feet of Jeff Cooper and his tireless proselytizing for the merits of the SA auto pistol as a defensive sidearm (usually to the detriment of the DA auto, by comparison). Cooper's thoughts on this subject have been so force-fully and brilliantly communicated that these days they have become the conventional wisdom, constantly repeated by shooters and instructors who are influenced, whether they know it or not, by his conclusions.

Let us pause for a moment to ponder a bit of alternate history. Just for the sake of argument, let's say that 40 years ago, when Jeff Cooper was quantifying many of the ideas on combat pistolcraft that are still accepted (with near-religious awe) by many American pistoleros even today, the only DA service autos in existence had *not* been war surplus Walther P.38s with egregious 18-pound DA trigger pulls or the new Smith & Wesson Model 39 (which was such a piece of crap it probably set back acceptance of the DA auto in America by about 15 years). What if Cooper had *liked* DA autos?

Fast forward to today, when Cooper's legacy of opinion regarding the DA auto (constantly repeated among shooters themselves in private discussions, read repeatedly in gun magazines, and taught by firearms instructors from the basic level onward) goes something like this: "The double-action auto gives you the best of both worlds. You've got the long, smooth, rolling trigger pull of a double-action revolver for the first shot, so you get a surprise trigger break for the utmost in accuracy. Thereafter the gun switches to SA to give you maximum speed for follow-up shots. You *can* have your cake and eat it, too!"

If new shooters heard *this* statement just before they first picked up a DA auto, do you really suppose they'd have so much trouble firing the thing? If you believe your gun is hard to shoot, it'll be hard to shoot. If, on the other hand, you regard it as an extremely easy piece to manage, the best system possibly available, then it will be much easier for you to fire well. Attitude is everything.

Having said all that, I will confess that I do believe the DA auto is a bit more challenging to shoot than the equivalent SA piece. That's because to fire a SA auto you only have to master one type of trigger pull. With the DA auto you've got to master three things: (1) DA shooting for your first shot, (2) SA shooting for all subsequent shots, and (3) instantly transitioning between the two.

It's a sad comment on the laziness of the average shooter, but watching other people fire DA autos on the range has convinced me that most people will never master these guns, because they sidestep the realization they must master three different types of shooting by practicing thusly: on the range, our typical shooter armed with a DA auto cranks off his first shot DA (and, since he's never practiced enough to become a good DA pistol shot, misses his point of aim widely); thereafter, he leaves the gun cocked in the SA mode for the rest of the shooting session! Frankly, in my opinion, if you carry a DA auto or rely on one for home defense, at least *half* your practice time should be spent on mastering the transition between the first and second trigger pulls.

Although the "crunch-tick" syndrome can indeed be very evident on the range among less well-trained shooters, I have to wonder just how much difference it makes for the purposes of real combat. I recall talking to Greg Hamilton just after he'd used a Simunitions-equipped SIG P226 to take on the Yavapai County SWAT team in a simulated gunfight at the National Tactical Invitationals. (And he did quite well, as a matter of fact. Practically got a standing ovation from the SWAT team after the "fight" was over!) Said Greg, "Some people say you'll screw up under stress if you're used to firing a gun like a Glock with a short, light trigger pull, and instead you have to use a gun with a double-action first shot. [Greg's normal carry gun is a Glock 19.] But when the ambushers started shooting at me, I don't even *remember* a double-action trigger pull on that SIG. And I certainly wasn't wasting any time going, 'Ah, yes, now I have to transition to a shorter trigger pull for the second shot.' As far as I was concerned, I wasn't holding a single-action auto or a double-action auto; it was just a *gun*, and I thought to myself, 'Hmmmmm, I have a gun in my hands—I should probably use it to fight with!'"

I've heard the argument, "Shooters who have been highly trained on single-action auto pistols tend to be the ones who really have problems with double-action autos. For instance, the finely honed skills of a Rob Leatham will be much more impacted by having to shoot a double-action auto than will those of the average duffer." Frankly, I doubt that. Once you become a Master Class IPSC shooter, you're good enough to kick anyone's ass shooting anything! It's only those people who are barely passable with a SA auto who fall to pieces when forced to shoot anything else.

All the foregoing doesn't mean that DA autos are for everyone. Consider the case of shooters who have insufficient hand strength to smoothly negotiate a long, heavy DA trigger pull. Folks in this category might include the elderly, small-statured men and women, and people with certain types of injuries or physical impediments. For these shooters, a gun with a short and light trigger pull is obviously the way to go, either a selective DA in the SA mode, or a dedicated SA auto to start with.

DA autos in general can present special problems for many female shooters. A woman may run into a couple of obstacles to good performance when firing these weapons that do not necessarily afflict her male counterpart. According to tests conducted by the U.S. Army and the Federal Law Enforcement Training Center (FLETC), the average woman has one-half to two-thirds the grip strength of the average man. Think about that for a second. With half the hand strength, a 12-pound DA trigger pull feels like 24 pounds to a woman. Also, according to FLETC data, the average woman's grip length (that's the distance from the center of the web of the shooting hand to the first joint of the trigger finger) is approximately one inch shorter than the average male hand. This means most women will not be able get enough of their trigger finger on a DA auto's forward-set trigger to negotiate the initial long, heavy trigger stroke with the gun properly centered in the shooting hand. I've seen women who simply couldn't make a DA auto *fire*, much less shoot it fast and accurately. Obviously, for many female shooters, a gun with a comparatively light trigger pull and a more rearward-set trigger, as on most SA pieces, would be far easier to handle.

All that is not to say that there aren't women who can handle DA autos. One of the most skillful female shooters of my personal acquaintance is my friend Dee Dee Orive, and her current carry gun is a DA SIG P228. Dee Dee's husband, Otto Orive, is a Kent, Washington, police officer and one of the firearms instructors for his department. Otto carries a SIG P220 .45 on duty and a P225 9mm while on his own time. Dee Dee has accompanied Otto and me many times when we've been shooting our SIGs against each other in some friendly competition/training sessions, so she had a lot of opportunities to watch DA autos being fired in skilled hands even before she decided to switch from a Colt Officer's ACP to a DA auto for her own carry piece. Dee Dee is herself a certified firearms instructor. She handles her SIG well.

It took some practice for Dee Dee to transition over to a very different gun design when she switched to the SIG from the SA .45 she'd been carrying. While she was in the process of getting grooved in on her new sidearm, Dee Dee told me, "Yeah, it's taking some work getting used to the double-action trigger pull on the SIG. I'm having trouble with my double taps. But I know it's possible to fire good double taps out of a double-action auto because I've been watching you and Otto do it for years!"

When I attended the aforementioned LFI-2 course, Dee Dee was also there as a class attendee. We were both armed with SIG P228s, and Dee Dee shot hers extremely well, firing that piece fast and accurately throughout the three-day course, all day long, every day. I was mightily impressed. There simply aren't that many women around with strong enough hands that they could do that. The P228 Dee Dee fired during this training was actually a loaner gun she had borrowed only shortly before the course; she didn't buy her own P228, one of the nickel-slide versions, until a couple of weeks later. I did think it was amusing when, after we'd fired the final double-speed qualification at the end of LFI-2 (this is the same course of fire as used in LFI-1, but the time limits are only half as long), Dee Dee and I compared our targets, both fired with P228s, and she said, "Wow, you really did great." I had scored 295 out of a possible 300 points, double-speed.

I said, "Well, what about you? God, you were awesome!"

To which Dee Dee replied, "Oh, no, I need a lot of practice. You shot much better than I did." Dee Dee had "only" scored a 293!

I would be misleading you, however, if I did not mention that Dee Dee has exceptionally strong hands for a woman, and her fingers are extraordinarily long. I'm not saying that DA autos are de facto out of the question for lady shooters. I *will* say that most female shooters, having as they do smaller and weaker hands than Dee Dee, would not be able to handle a DA auto nearly as nicely as she does.

So, if DA autos are not for everyone, let's consider some alternatives. The first, obviously, would be a SA auto. Also, there are numerous auto designs out there that give you the option of SA cocked-and-locked carry, or DA starting with the hammer down on a round in the chamber, the so-called "selective double actions." (I would go so far as to say that, for my own use, on these guns I would almost invariably choose the cocked-and-locked mode of carry for the maximum ease of shooting.) And, as previously discussed, for some people it may be a desirable thing to have the short, light SA trigger pull for every shot, including the first one, and a rearward-set trigger versus the DA gun's long trigger reach, simply so they can fire the gun!

The new breed of "double-action-only" (DAO) autoloaders that have made their appearance over the past few years, like DA revolvers, possess a long, accidental-discharge-resistant DA trigger pull for each and every shot. (As a matter of fact, these guns were first developed in response to requests from police departments wanting "higher firepower revolvers.") Although many gun shop commandos are down on DAO autos as somehow being not "cool," these guns can perform their intended mission well in competent hands. The DAO autos' long DA trigger pulls give them a very rhythmic trigger action and a surprise trigger break that can allow shooters to fire quite accurately, and fairly swiftly as well, once the guns are mastered. That's the good news. The bad news is there's no switching over to the light, easy-handlin' SA trigger pull after the first shot, as on conventional DA autos. Oh, well . . . there ain't no such thing as a free lunch!

SUMMARY

The DA auto *is* a bit more challenging to master than some other types of semiautos, but acquiring real proficiency with one of these guns is hardly the equivalent of performing brain surgery while wearing kitchen mittens that champions of the SA auto pistol would have you believe it is.

It may be argued with considerable logic that the DA auto is the best general-purpose auto pistol trigger system. The DA auto's long, heavy initial trigger pull provides the resistance to accidental discharge (and correspondingly greater safety in high stress gunpoint situations) of a DA revolver, while the short, light trigger pulls for all succeeding shots provide the enhanced hit potential of a SA auto, all in the same gun. The best of both worlds? For most people . . . absolutely!

CHAPTER THREE

HANDGUN STOPPING POWER

Virginia, your little friends are wrong. . . . Not believe in Santa Claus? You might as well not believe in fairies.

—Francis Pharcellus Church
"Is There a Santa Claus?"
(first published in *The New York Sun* on September 21, 1897,
in reply to an inquiry from Virginia O'Hanlon)

Perhaps the greatest myth in the firearms field is that of handgun stopping power. When you first start getting into handguns, you'll often hear people (all of whom seem to know more about the topic than you) tossing around the term "stopping power" as if was going out of style and they had to use it up quick, usually in sentences that go something like this: "Well, everyone knows a .45 auto has more stopping power than a 9mm." Or how about this one: "Yeah, in .40 S&W caliber I think the 155-grain ammo definitely has more stopping power than the 180-grain stuff." What the hell are they talking about? What exactly is "stopping power," and how do you get it?

This is a question rivaling "Does God exist, and if so what is he/she/it like?" for generating weighty pronouncements, rigidly held and jealously defended opinions, and total resistance to a definitive answer. For practical purposes, stopping power can be defined as that quality in a handgun projectile that forces a violent attacker to cease aggressive action when hit with it. Many folks are understandably terrified of the possibility of homicidal criminal attack, and they want to *know* that if they hit their opponent with a minimum of handgun bullets (preferably one) they will instantly shut down the threat to their lives. For some, this can become well nigh an obsession. And so the ammo companies are constantly introducing "new and improved" handgun projectiles, all with the goal of giving the defensive shooter more of that elusive quality called stopping power.

In this chapter, I am not going to tell you which handgun calibers are the best "stoppers." Nor am I going to recommend particular brands or makes of ammo within the various calibers. Rather, I'm going to address the facts leading me to conclude that things like this are really rather unimportant.

To have a commonsense discussion of stopping power, we first need to understand a few things, such as why some people stop when shot, why some people don't stop, as well as common theories of stopping power. Let's start with why people stop.

WHY PEOPLE STOP

There are three reasons why someone you've just been forced to shoot might stop what he's doing (such as trying to kill you). These are (1) a psychological reaction to being shot, (2) a neurological reaction to being shot, or (3) blood pressure loss. Let's take these in order.

Reason #1: Psychological Reaction to Being Shot

Former Detroit Police Detective Evan Marshall has analyzed the results of thousands of real-life gunfights. Marshall notes that, 40 to 50 percent of the time, people who are shot instantly cease all aggressive action, even when hit in places that should not have been disabling. In other words, they stop if they get hit *anywhere* with *anything*. The only way to explain this is as a psychological reaction to being shot. Basically, the person who's just been shot says to himself, "Oh, I've been shot. I should probably give up or fall down." The classic case of this phenomenon is the young cop who was hit in the arm with a single round of .25 ACP (the absolute lowest-powered handgun cartridge in common usage). He looked down, saw that he was shot, and literally dropped dead from a wound not much more serious than if he were hit with a pellet gun! Consciously or subconsciously, he had programmed himself that if he was ever shot it would result in his death. He was shot, and he died!

Why certain people should have such reactions and other people not is a subject of intense debate. Some commentators point to the influence of TV and movies, where a shot from a .38 snubbie sends the bad guy flying 50 feet through the air and out a plate-glass window, which tends to give the average person the belief that handguns are much more powerful than they actually are. It's also an undeniable fact that some people are just wimps; the pain of being hit with a bullet anywhere is enough to make them stop what they're doing.

Now, the good news is that, according to Marshall, about half the time if we hit our opponent anywhere with anything, he'll have a psychological reaction that forces him to stop. The bad news is that this reaction is at the option of the opponent: he can also choose not to stop.

Reason #2: Neurological Reaction to Being Shot

Basically, we're talking here about interrupting a person's central nervous system, i.e., shooting him in the spine or brain.

To start with, we can forget the spine as a stopping zone, unless you plan on shooting people in the back. In most police and civilian self-defense shootings, the attacker is facing the defender, which means the bullet would have to course through the entire body without deflecting and still retain enough energy to break the protecting spine, and then cut the spinal cord. That sort of bullet performance simply can't be expected from a handgun projectile. For one thing, bullets have a tendency to do all sorts of strange things inside the human body rather than travel in a straight line: they tumble, they carom off bones, they go off in different directions simply from the force of flesh and liquids on their trajectory. You can't just aim at your attacker's midline and figure you're going to punch a bullet through him to his spine.

Also, after traversing the entire body cavity, there are very few handgun bullets that would still have enough energy left to penetrate the protecting spine and sever the spinal cord. With high-powered rifles, it's another story—simply coming close to the spine will often dislocate vertebrae solely from the pressure wave of the projectile passing through flesh. Often, dislodged vertebrae themselves will cut the spinal cord whether the bullet touches the spine or not. However, that simply doesn't happen with handgun bullets.

So if you can't hit the spine, what's left? You might be able to hit the brain. But again, we have some good and bad news. The good news is that if you hit the brain, it will usually stop your attacker definitively, disconnect his electrical system, and drop him dead in his tracks. The bad news is that doing so requires making an extremely difficult shot. Hit your opponent anywhere above the eyebrows and the bullet will almost certainly ricochet off the hard, thick, convex cranium. Hit him below the cheekbones, and it's highly unlikely you'll get full penetration—you've got to deal with a heavy upper and lower jawbone and hard enamel teeth set up at weird angles, all of which can stop or deflect a handgun bullet. Even if you did manage to make your way through all that heavy bone, below the cheekbones there's almost nothing worthwhile to hit. The vast majority of the human brain is up high, inside the well-protected cranial vault. Lower than that, and all you've got is the brain stem, which is about an inch wide.

In order to make a "head shot" work, you'd have to slip a bullet through the eye sockets or the nasal septum. On a full-grown man, this is a target area approximately two inches high by four inches wide. In the real world, under stress, in bad lighting, with both you and your opponent moving (all of which are possible, if not probable), making that sort of shot is going to be very difficult. It will require a higher degree of shooting skill than most people possess. It's not that shots like this can't be made, it's just that most people can't shoot well enough under stress to count on the head shot as a reliable stopper.

Reason #3: Blood Pressure Loss

Okay, the psychological reaction to being shot is unreliable because it's at the option of the opponent. The neurological reaction to a spine or brain shot, although it will usually stop an aggressor cold, probably cannot be counted on in an emergency. We're left with only one other thing that might make our attacker stop, and that is blood pressure loss. This is the only guarantee we have: if we put enough holes in the guy, eventually his body's hydraulic system is going to fail from lack of fluid. Unfortunately, waiting for an attacker to run out of blood can take a little longer than most people want to wait if the person in question is trying to kill them.

• • •

The bottom line is, the reasons people stop are largely beyond your control and have very little, if anything, to do with the caliber of your defensive handgun or the ammunition with which you load it.

Now that we've discussed reasons people stop, let us address why people don't stop.

WHY PEOPLE DON'T STOP

There are four reasons why people don't stop when shot: (1) body armor, (2) drugs, (3) adrenaline, and (4) you missed. Let's take these in order.

Reason #1: Body Armor

It's possible your attacker might be wearing bullet-resistant body armor. It's *highly* unlikely, but it's possible. During the famous Brinks robbery in Nyack, New York, a police sergeant armed with a .38 revolver center-punched one of the robbers to no effect, only to be killed later himself. His bullet had been stopped by the criminal's Kevlar vest. When the cop killer was later slain by police, they found the flattened-out .38 slug in a pocket, put there as a souvenir.

Still, for all the time some people spend worrying about things like this, it's really a very unrealistic concern. It is extremely unlikely your attacker will be wearing body armor. When I discussed this matter with Richard Davis, president of Second Chance Body Armor and the inventor, 25 years ago, of concealable "bulletproof vests," he told me that the above-mentioned New York shooting is the only incident of which he's aware where a good guy was ever killed because the opposition had body armor (not a Second Chance vest, by the way; Second Chance sells its products only to police, military personnel, and civilians who can provide proof of a clean criminal background). Hmmmmm, once in 25 years. Those are pretty good odds!

Reason #2: Drugs

Many people worry about running into an opponent so high on drugs he simply doesn't notice he's been shot. Although there have been horrific incidents that prove this can indeed happen, they are so rare as to be extraordinary when they do occur. There's one thing most people seem to overlook when obsessing about this eventuality: most serious junkies are pretty sad physical specimens, debilitated by their addictions. When they're not high they're in such pitiful shape, weak and shaking, that if anything, they're *more* likely to go down if shot. And when they are high, when they've got their drug, all is right with the world. Heroin freaks, crackheads, and most other addicts are not going to waste their high time *working*, placing themselves under stress, by going out and trying to rob and kill people. It's when they're *not* high that they'll try to rob and kill to get money for their drugs. And, as previously mentioned, when he's not high, a serious addict is in such pathetic physical shape that he's actually more likely than most opponents to go down.

The only drugs of which I'm aware that might generate aggression and make an attacker oblivious to being shot with a handgun would be PCP and methamphetamines. Thankfully, these are not popular drugs. The chances of your ever running into a human bullet sponge who soaks up round after round because he's high on drugs are very slight.

However, the most commonly encountered drug on the street is alcohol, which frequently does result in an aggressive attacker and is also notorious for damping out a person's responses to being shot. An opponent under the influence of alcohol can be oblivious to the pain of a gunshot wound. They don't call it "feeling no pain" for nothing!

Reason #3: Adrenaline

Let's say you've just shot a homicidal criminal a few times high up in the chest with a decent handgun load . . . he ignores it and keeps attacking. Why would something like that happen? Probably because he's so pumped up and supercharged with adrenaline he simply doesn't *care* that you've shot him, at least for the moment.

If you are ever attacked by a mugger, burglar, rapist, or other criminal intent on killing or seriously injuring you, he will have a great advantage over you in that he has had prior warning of the impending fight. While you have to react from a condition of peace, your opponent almost always has been planning the crime for a period of time prior to the conflict. This has given his body time to produce enormous quantities of adrenaline as it readies itself for the fight.

So there you are, walking along thinking about your wife or girlfriend (or husband or boyfriend, if you're a lady) or what you're going to have for dinner, while your opponent has, for all practical purposes, been in combat for 5, 10, 20 minutes, with all the adrenaline flow that entails. Once an attacker is pumped up with heavy adrenaline flow, there is frequently little reaction to being shot with a handgun. There are many instances on record where people in the middle of a fight-or-die situation have been shot and not even realized they'd been hit until someone pointed the fact out to them later!

A person pumped up on adrenaline can be superhuman in his resistance to pain and injury. Adrenaline is the most powerful hormone produced by the body. They inject this stuff into heart attack patients to bring the dead back to life. An attacker high on adrenaline can be a terrifying opponent, quite capable of ignoring lethal hits with a handgun, or even a high-powered rifle or shotgun, long enough to kill you. Some macho morons will say, "Well, at least I'll have the satisfaction of knowing I took the bastard with me." I'm not impressed with their logic. I don't want to "take the bastard with me." I'd rather have him go on ahead while I stay behind. Alive.

Reason #4: You Missed

When an armed good guy shoots at a homicidal attacker and the bad guy continues trying to kill him, the single most common reason for that sad state of affairs is that the good guy missed. Most cops and civilian gun carriers are *lousy* handgun shots. The level of ineptitude of many people who carry guns on a daily basis is nothing short of appalling.

I have a lot of respect for many police officers and the very difficult, sometimes heroic job they do, but I do get a little tired of people, both cops and civilians, who assume that wearing a uniform automatically makes a person a gun expert. Here are a few facts for you: of all the police officers shot annually, 50 percent shoot themselves. I'm not talking suicides here; I'm talking about accidentally putting a bullet into their own bodies. Fortunately, these injuries are rarely fatal, as they consist mostly of gunshot wounds to the off-hand while drawing or a bullet to the strong-side leg while reholstering. Another 30 percent of police officers shot are accidentally shot by other cops. Another 10 percent are shot with their own guns after being disarmed by other people. Obviously, this is not expert-level performance. Now, there are police officers out there who are very weapons knowledgeable. I know a few like that. However, they are greatly in the minority. And most civilian gun carriers are just as incompetent as most cops.

The vast majority of people don't have the skill level necessary to swiftly and accurately put their bullets where they'll do the most good in a defensive emergency. This is, in my opinion, the single greatest cause of "stopping power failures."

(I might mention in passing that you shouldn't think you can't be a good handgun shot just because you're not an "expert" like a cop or soldier. We've already addressed the skill level you can expect of the average police officer. And take it from someone who spent 10 years in the U.S. Army, three of them as an Airborne paratrooper: Army marksmanship standards gum the big one. A serious civilian shooter can be far, far better than the average policeman or soldier.)

• • •

So, the reasons people don't stop are also largely beyond your control and have very little, if anything, to do with your handgun's caliber or ammunition. The only thing over which you really have control is whether or not you miss.

TYPES OF WOUNDING

There are two types of wounding that can be caused by firearms: high-velocity and low-velocity. High-velocity wounding occurs with high-powered rifles and short-range shotgun blasts. Low-velocity wounding occurs with handguns and medium- to long-range shotgun blasts. Let's discuss these two very different types of wounding.

High-Velocity Wounding

The tissue that is actually touched and destroyed by a projectile (the bullet hole, in other words) is called by wound ballisticians the permanent wound cavity. In high-velocity wounding, most of the damage is not actually caused by the permanent wound cavity, but rather by the large area of disrupted flesh surrounding the path of the bullet. To understand why this occurs, keep in mind that the human body is composed mostly of water, and then picture tossing a pebble into a pond. The water ripples and moves, even far from where the pebble hits. When an extremely high velocity projectile passes through human tissue, the pressure wave from the bullet causes the flesh to actually be pushed away from its path. This is called the temporary wound channel, because the tissue collapses back down after the pressure wave abates—the temporary wound channel actually exists for only a minute fraction of a second. With high-velocity projectiles, the movement of flesh as the pressure wave blasts it open to create the temporary wound channel happens so swiftly and violently that it overstresses the tissue and causes it to disrupt. If you've ever seen a deer that's been hit with a high-powered rifle, you know what I'm talking about. You've got a small hole in the flesh surrounded by a big area of pulped tissue; it looks like raspberry jelly.

Now, at what speed does a projectile start to cause high-velocity wounding? According to the U.S. Army, which has done considerable testing in this area, you begin to get high-velocity wounding effects at projectile speeds more than 2,500 feet per second (fps). This is why high-powered rifles are so much more destructive than handguns. You simply don't get high-velocity wounding with hand-

THE TRUTH ABOUT HANDGUNS

gun bullets because there are no handgun projectiles that move this fast. For our purposes that leaves us with low-velocity wounding

Low-Velocity Wounding

In high-velocity wounding, the majority of the damage is caused by the temporary wound channel. In low-velocity wounding, most of the damage is done by the permanent wound cavity. There is a certain amount of temporary wound channel with handgun bullets. However, the tissue moves so slowly, relatively speaking, that the flesh does not disrupt, but instead snaps back into place, stretched, hurting, torn, perhaps, but still functional.

• • •

For all practical purposes, we may classify a close-range shotgun blast, where all the pellets are touching or nearly touching each other when they impact flesh, as high-velocity wounding. Although shotgun blasts travel so slowly they are technically low velocity, at close range they cause high-velocity-wounding-type effects. You see, each individual shotgun pellet is a low-velocity projectile that creates its own permanent wound cavity and small temporary wound channel. By themselves, these smallish temporary wound channels are no big deal, but when at close range the pellets hit flesh simultaneously while almost touching, the tiny pressure waves from each pellet flow across each other, amplify, and you get tissue disruption like high-velocity wounding. Wound ballisticians and medical examiners call the results of a point-blank shotgun blast a "rat hole" wound, because that's what it looks like. We're talking a fist-sized hole punched through the human body here, folks. This is why the shotgun has such a terrifying reputation as a short-range manstopper. At longer distances (much more than 10 feet), as the shotgun pellets spread out and the temporary wound channels are no longer touching each other, this effect goes away, and instead of high-velocity wounding you get a bunch of low-velocity wounds.

So, what does all this talk of high-powered rifles and shotguns have to do with handgun stopping power? I've discussed high-velocity wounding and the effects of rifle bullets and short-range shotgun blasts for a reason. You see, even with the horrific wounds delivered by rifles and shotguns, these weapons are not 100-percent reliable manstoppers. There are many cases of determined assailants taking multiple shots from high-powered rifles, and even 12-gauge shotgun blasts, and continuing to attack. When you consider this, the discussion of handgun "stopping power" assumes the proportions of a bad joke.

Handguns are inherently anemic firearms that are much less powerful than the truly serious weapons. The only thing handguns really have going for them as weapons is their small size, with its resultant portability, concealability, and maneuverability. In other words, unlike a bulky rifle or shotgun, a handgun can *be there* when you need it. In return for that compact size and portability, the handgun sacrifices any great measure of power. Handgun stopping power is a myth.

There's simply no way to get much real power into something as small as a handgun cartridge. This was first pointed out to me by nationally famous firearms instructor John Farnam. After talking to Farnam, I went home, took a round of .45 auto ammo (a caliber with a legendary reputation for stopping power), laid it out on a table, and placed my hand down next to it. "The mighty, manstopping .45." And suddenly, I realized something: the entire *cartridge* was about the size of the first joint on my little finger! That kind of put things in perspective for me.

So, the caliber for which your defensive handgun is chambered is really rather unimportant. No matter whether your defense gun is a .380 ACP, a .38 Special or .357 Magnum, a 9mm, .40 S&W or .45 ACP, it's still going to be, in the overall scheme of things, wimpy. For all the tons of ink expended writing on the topic of handgun stopping power and all the research and development on improved handgun projectiles, there remains that one undeniable fact: all handguns are seriously underpowered for the job of stopping a determined assailant.

As we know from our previous discussion, the reasons people stop are largely beyond our control. The reasons people don't stop are also largely beyond our control. The only thing we can really control is whether or not we miss. If we can't control the reasons people stop, and we can't control the reasons they don't stop, then the only way we can increase the likelihood of halting our opponent is to hit him in the right spots, to deliver what little wounding power the handgun does possess where it will do the most good, and thus maximize the damage our bullets do.

Does it really matter at all what ammunition you choose to load into your defense gun? Well, yes. If you're shooting an auto pistol, I believe you should make feed reliability a top priority. Ammunition that has a rounded, ball-shaped ogive to it will be far more reliable than bullets that have flat-nose, truncated-cone, or semi-wadcutter shapes. I also don't like any handgun load for self-defense that will predictably punch all the way through the human body, for reasons I'll get into later. Choose a load that has wound ballistics you like, with whatever combination of penetration, bullet expansion, or whatnot that meets your fancy. Then *forget about it* and start practicing, concentrating on becoming such a good pistol shot that you can swiftly hit a homicidal attacker fast, hard, and repeatedly.

A GREATLY ABBREVIATED DISCUSSION ON THEORIES OF STOPPING POWER

I could take this space to address all the various mathematical models proposed to predict stopping power put forth for the last century, reams of anecdotal shooting results, testing bullet performance in ballistic gelatin, the theoretical effects of bore size on stopping power, etc. You'll be relieved to hear I'm not going to do that. Let's get this down to the real nitty-gritty. The basic goal behind attempts to improve handgun stopping power is to increase the amount of damage a handgun bullet does to the human body. When all is said and done, there are really only a few theories on how to do this.

Let's assume for a moment, just for the sake of argument, that some handgun calibers do cause more damage to the human body than others, and that some loads within certain calibers—through a combination of bullet design, construction, and velocity—are more destructive than some other loads. How do you make a bullet do more damage? There are basically two moderately effective ways, and one *really* effective way, to achieve this goal.

The first way to cause more damage with a handgun bullet is to go to a larger bullet and tear a wider wound channel. You can achieve this either by starting with a big bullet and/or by expanding a hollowpointed bullet. All the development in expanding bullets, hypervelocity hollowpoints, etc., over the past 30 years has been aimed at this goal, making bullets tear bigger holes as they travel through the human body. Of course, you can't make a bullet *that* much bigger, and remember, no matter how much your projectile expands, it's still a wimpy handgun bullet. This approach to increasing stopping power is moderately effective.

People who go for the expanding-bullet approach to hyping up stopping power speak knowledgeably of "energy dump," i.e., that a bullet which does not penetrate all the way through the human body dumps all its energy there and, therefore, causes more trauma to the nervous system. (You see, the more a bullet expands, the wider its frontal area becomes, the greater the drag on the projectile as it travels through the body, and the less it penetrates.) If the bullet totally penetrates the body, any energy not "dumped" inside the body cavity, so the theory goes, is wasted. To be honest, I never quite figured this one out: it always seemed to me that it takes more energy to punch a bullet all the way through a body than not, and the shock to the nervous system from that greater energy would increase correspondingly. Anyway, it's a moot point: handgun projectiles are so low-powered that there's really not that much kinetic energy there to "dump" anyway.

Having a bullet that does not totally penetrate your opponent's body is, however, a very good thing for reasons that have nothing to do with stopping power. Any projectile that overpenetrates is a potential wild shot that could possibly hit and kill an innocent person. The only safe stopping place for your bullets is inside the body of the criminal who forced you to shoot him.

The second theory on how to increase the amount of damage a bullet does is to make the projectile penetrate more deeply, therefore puncturing more vital organs and blood vessels. Usually, this is accomplished by retarding expansion. As previously mentioned, when a bullet expands, its increased frontal area results in greater drag, causing it to penetrate less deeply. On the other hand, *less* expansion equals *deeper* penetration. The problem with this, of course, is that you wind up with dangerous overpenetration. Frankly, I'd have a hard time living with myself if I knowingly chose over-penetrative ammo for my handgun and then killed an innocent person who happened to be standing, unseen, behind my attacker.

Those experts who believe penetration is the way to go in a handgun bullet and those who believe expansion is the ticket are mortal enemies. Frankly, I remain unimpressed by either argument. Neither increased expansion nor increased penetration is going to make your handgun do the job of a high-powered rifle or a shotgun.

For years I've been referring, semifacetiously I thought, to "people who'll promise you that, with the right caliber and load, a handgun will give you stopping power more in line with a buckshot-loaded 12-gauge." Well, believe it or not, that's really true! Read Evan Marshall and Ed Sanow's *Street Stoppers* for the following statistics: Remington 12-gauge 3-inch Magnum double-ought buckshot, one-shot stopping power—94 percent (that's with at least 9 of the 12 pellets hitting the thoracic cavity). Federal .357 Magnum 125-grain jacketed hollowpoint (JHP), one-shot stopping power—96 percent. Let's think about that for a second. Three-inch Magnum buckshot gives us at least *nine* .33-caliber projectiles, moving approximately 1,200 fps out of a shorty "riot gun" barrel, hitting the torso at once. The 125-grain .357 gives us one .36-caliber projectile, traveling about 1,450 fps out of a 4-inch barrel. But the handgun bullet has *more* stopping power than the shotgun load. Yeah, I know if *my* life depended on sledging down some miscreant, I'd dump the 12-gauge loaded with 3-inch Magnums in the dirt and draw my revolver. Wouldn't you?

This brings us to our third way to increase the damage our handgun bullets do. Those people who believe you can graph handgun stopping power (on actuarial tables that look like they came from an insurance agent!) will choose a particular load based on a claimed advantage of a few percentage points. Well, I'm going to tell you a way to *double* your handgun bullet's effectiveness. However much damage your bullet does, however big a hole it rips, however much it expands, however deeply it penetrates, there is one thing that will absolutely, positively, guaranteed cause 100-percent more damage:

Another hole.

If someone is trying to kill you, shoot him as accurately and swiftly as possible and *keep shooting*, as many times as necessary. Only stop when he stops . . . trying to kill you, that is. It's really the only way to predictably, swiftly terminate the threat to your life.

This, of course, is the kicker, because most shooters don't have a high enough level of skill to pull off that sort of marksmanship. Which is why we have the frenzied search for a more effective handgun bullet. Knowing his skill level sucks, the average shooter says to himself, "Okay, I've got 18 rounds in my Glock. If I'm lucky I may be able to hit my opponent once before I run out of ammo. I need a bullet so good that one hit will drop him like a felled steer." It's pathetic. Our example shooter doesn't need a wonderbullet; he needs to learn how to shoot. But that means practicing until his skills improve. It's always easier to improve technology than to improve people, and so we'll continue to try to find ways to make the technology compensate for lack of skill on the shooter's part.

The only "stopping power" you can really control is your own level of skill with your defensive firearm. Hit your opponent in the right places, hit him hard, hit him fast, hit him repeatedly . . . and what you hit him *with* will be largely immaterial.

AUTHOR'S NOTE: Many of the ideas on stopping power presented in this chapter came from other people. There's not much of this stuff that I made up myself. I'm not that perceptive. This all comes from master firearms instructors like Greg Hamilton and John Farnam far more than from Duane Thomas. I was first exposed to a lot of the ideas addressed in this chapter when I attended the lecture portion of Greg Hamilton's Advanced Handguns Skills course at his firearms school, InSights Training Center, in Washington state. (I feel very fortunate that I managed to capture Greg's lecture on tape, and I was so impressed that I actually made it one of the segments on the first volume of *The Gun Expert's Video Library*, my firearms video magazine.) I just wanted to give credit where it's due.

ALVIN YORK: HERO WITH A .45 AUTO

Heroism feels and never reasons and therefore is always right.
— Ralph Waldo Emerson
Essays: First Series, "Heroism"

One of the most incredible stories of heroism and individual feats of arms in the modern age occurred during World War I in the Argonne Forest of France on October 8, 1918. On that day, then-Corporal Alvin C. York, essentially single-handedly, whipped an entire German machine gun battalion, killed 28 enemy soldiers, and, with the help of a handful of doughboys, captured and brought in 132 prisoners. This feat was called by France's Marshal Foch, "the greatest thing accomplished by any private soldier of all the armies of Europe." (We pause to note that as an American soldier, York was *not* a member of the armies of Europe . . . but you get the general idea.)

The reason a chapter on these events is appearing in a book on handguns is that (or so we are told) at one time during that bloody day's work, Corporal York used a .45 auto to stop a German squad bayonet charge, an act held in near-religious awe by devotees of the single-action Model of 1911 as proof positive of this handgun's efficiency as a battle weapon. Despite the fact that most handgunners are vaguely aware that some such event took place, there is widespread confusion about exactly what happened that historic day in 1918. For one thing, the number of German soldiers involved in the bayonet charge is variously cited as five, six, or seven. Also, it has been stated that York shot most of the enemy soldiers charging him with his rifle, only turning to the pistol to finish off the last few men when the long gun was empty. In this chapter, we'll set the record straight.

Since I hate operating on hearsay in any matter, I decided to do some investigation. Primary among my research materials was the 1928 book, *Sergeant York, His Own Life Story and War Diary*, edited by York's friend, journalist Tom Skeyhill. You see, York kept a diary during his wartime service in Europe. (This was highly against regulations, by the way. In case a soldier was taken prisoner, the Army did not want a captured diary providing important information to the enemy. A stubborn individualist, York went so far as to refuse to give the diary to his commanding officer when asked for it, stating, "I didn't come to the war to be captured.") As you would expect, the entries in a diary kept by a war-weary serviceman are, of course, brief. What Skeyhill did in the York "autobiography" was to reprint York's war diary, in situ, but in between the diary entries are York's detailed verbal statements and amplifications on those often terse passages.

It's a fascinating book, in part because the "verbal" passages are in dialect. The reason dialect (putting forth an individual's dialogue in such a way as to give the impression of a particular accent) is so out of favor in modern literary circles is that it's very hard to do well, and if done poorly it's almost unreadable. However, Skeyhill does a good job of it; his use of dialect when transcribing York's statements calls forth a very real sense of York's personality. (Skeyhill, although reprinting the war diary unchanged, did take it upon himself to clean up the largely uneducated York's spelling in the verbally dictated portions of the book: thus, York's "german magor" from his war diary becomes a "German major" a few paragraphs later.)

But enough of that. Alvin Cullum York was born December 13, 1887, in a one-room log cabin in the Valley of the Three Forks of the Wolf River in the Cumberland Mountains of Tennessee. With the exception of time out to become a legend during his military service in Europe, York spent almost his entire 76 years (1887–1964) in this land. Alvin York was an unlikely hero who reported for military service only after his repeated attempts to win a deferment on religious grounds failed. York was a conscientious objector! (The 1941 Gary Cooper film *Sergeant York* deals primarily with the extremely devout mountain man's attempts to reconcile the religious injunction against killing with his nation's call to war.) Physically, York was red-headed, freckle-faced, tall and sturdy, a six-footer, broad-shouldered, deep-chested, with gunmetal blue-gray eyes.

Speaking of guns, they were a major part of York's boyhood. He began using weapons when very small and almost couldn't recall a time when he hadn't owned a gun. In the hard Tennessee hills, making a shot on game was often no mere matter of sport; it meant feeding yourself and your family, and Alvin York reported to U.S. Army service already a superlative marksman.

York was assigned to Company G, 2nd Battalion, 328th Infantry Regiment, 82nd Division, a combat unit destined for front-line service. Originally composed of recruits from Georgia, Alabama, and Tennessee, the 82nd eventually came to include men from every state in the union. In recognition of this diversity, it was nicknamed the "All-American" division, a name that endures to the present time. (Today, this unit is the famed 82nd Airborne Division.)

During basic training York had become quite impressed with his issue rifle (although he noted with pride that it was no more accurate than his old muzzle-loading "squirrel gun"). But when he got to Europe, the Army withdrew his unit's Springfield 1903s and issued as replacements British-designed but American-made 1917 Enfields chambered for 30.06—the Springfields were, apparently, in turn distributed to foreign allies! (The ways of military organizations are, as always, wondrous to behold.) York found it painful to give up a weapon he had already begun to think of as a friend.

The story of the military maneuvering of Allied and German units in wartime Europe, necessary to bring Alvin York to his appointment with destiny, could comprise a chapter all its own. Suffice it to say that on October 8, 1918, the 2nd Battalion was moving through a valley in the French Argonne Forest. Unknown to the

Americans, German machine guns had a fine position occupying the high ground above them on three sides. When York's unit reached the middle of the valley, the point of maximum exposure, the hills around them exploded. From the right, the high ground of Champocher Ridge, and from the left, a heavily wooded hill, poured down machine gun fire and mortar shells. American soldiers died en masse; the survivors flung themselves into mortar holes or any other available cover.

With the forward platoons pinned down, the decision was made to send three squads of men to the left side to attack the machine gun emplacements firing down on the Americans from the wooded hill. Depleted by casualties, the three squads totaled only 16 men, instead of the usual 24. These squads were led by Sgt. Bernard Early; one of his men was Cpl. Alvin York. The Americans slipped around the left flank and advanced approximately 1 1/2 miles through the dense forest before suddenly coming upon two Germans wearing Red Cross arm bands. One man surrendered, but the other fled, with the American patrol hot after him.

In pursuit of this fellow, Early and his men came out of the brush onto a group of several dozen German soldiers having breakfast who, exhausted from a night of marching, had dropped their belts and weapons to the ground. The Americans were almost as surprised as the Germans . . . but that didn't stop them from opening fire on the enemy soldiers, most of whom promptly surrendered. When one soldier kept firing, York had to kill him. Then, suddenly, the clearing was swept by machine guns hidden on a hill behind the camp. Huddled in the center of the clearing, the Germans dropped safely to the ground, but fully half the American soldiers were killed in the first few seconds. Sergeant Early and one corporal were hit, while a second corporal, York's best friend, Murray Savage, was killed outright, his clothes shot to shreds by what is estimated as more than a hundred bullets.

Standing to the left of the prisoners, York fell to the ground. Bullets chewed up the terrain around him. A nearby shrapnel helmet was "all sorter sieved, jes like the top of a pepper box," as York put it. Trapped in the open between the German prisoners and the blazing machine guns on the hill, armed only with a bolt-action battle rifle and a .45 auto, Alvin York began to fight back!

His fellow soldiers pinned down or seeking cover, York was one man against a machine gun nest. No enviable task; however, fate had conspired to deal the embattled corporal a few kind cards. He was so close to the enemy machine gunners that they had to depress their fire to hit him and so close to the German prisoners that the gunners had to look before firing or risk killing their own men. When they raised up to take aim, the veteran of many a Tennessee turkey shoot just blew them away, one after another. When a head would pop up to take a look, York shot it. Quoting from *Sergeant York, His Own Life Story and War Diary*:

> As soon as I was able I stood up and begun to shoot off-hand, which is my favourite position. I was still sharpshooting with that-there old army rifle. I used up several clips. The barrel was getting hot and my rifle ammunition was running low, or was where it was hard for me to get at it quickly. But I had to keep on shooting jes the same.
>
> In the middle of the fight a German officer and five men done jumped out of a trench and charged me with fixed bayonets. They had about twenty-five yards to come and they were coming right smart. I only had about half a clip left in my rifle; but I had my pistol ready. I done flipped it out fast and teched them off, too.
>
> I teched off the sixth man first; then the fifth; then the fourth; then the third; and so on. That's the way we shoot wild turkeys at home. You see we don't want the front ones to know that we're getting the back ones, and then they keep on coming until we get them all. Of course, I hadn't time to think of that. I guess I jes naturally did it. I knowed, too, that if the front ones wavered, or if I stopped them the rear ones would drop down and pump a volley into me and get me.

Apparently the Germans, knowing York was armed with a rifle with a five-round clip, had hoped at least one of the six men would be able to get to the American sharpshooter before he could reload. Down to "about half a clip" in his service rifle, York turned to the pistol instead to finish the skirmish. So, it *is* true that Alvin York stopped a German bayonet charge of six men using his Colt 1911 .45 auto! Describing the reactions of the men hit with his .45, York said he shot "the lieutenant right through the stomach and he dropped and squealed like a pig. All the Boches who were hit squealed just like pigs." (Hardly the instantaneous, sterile "one shot stops" painted by proselytizing .45 auto fanatics, by the way. Reality tends to be a bit more messy.) But the fight wasn't over:

> Then I returned to the rifle, and kept right on after those machine guns. I knowed now that if I done kept my head and didn't run out of ammunition I had them. So I done hollered to them to come down and give up. I didn't want to kill any more'n I had to. I would tech a couple of them off and holler again. But I guess they couldn't understand my language, or else they couldn't hear me in that awful racket that was going on all around. Over twenty Germans were killed by this time.

In the middle of battle and carnage, there can emerge some strikingly funny moments. The German ranking officer, a First Lieutenant Vollmer (not, as York thought, a major . . . or even a "magor") had worked in Chicago before the war and spoke excellent English. The battle with the machine gunners finally ended when, as York relates:

> I got hold of a german magor and he told me if I wouldn't kill any more of them he would make them quit firing . . . I think he had done been firing at me while I was fighting the machine guns—I examined his pistol later and sure enough hit was empty. Jes the same, he hadn't pestered me nohow. After he seed me stop the six Germans who charged with fixed bayonets he got up off the ground and walked over to me and yelled "English?"
> I said, "No, not English."
> He said, "What?"
> I said, "American."
> He said, "Good Lord!"

The German officer offered to order his men to surrender . . . if

York wouldn't kill any more of them! Vollmer had already watched York survive the machine gunners' initial assault, the squad bayonet charge, and (in all probability) Vollmer's own attempt to kill him, all apparently without missing a single shot himself, and the German officer had seen enough. York did, however, have to kill two more Germans with his .45 that day. As he recounts, continuing on in his conversation with Vollmer:

> Then he said, "If you won't shoot any more I will make them give up."
> I told him he had better. I covered him with my automatic and told him if he didn't make them stop firing I would take his head next. And he knowed I meaned it. So he blowed a little whistle and they come down out of the trench and throwed down their guns and equipment and held up their hands and begun to gather around. I guess, though, one of them thought he could get me. He had his hands up all right. But he done had a little hand grenade concealed, and as he come up to me he throwed it right at my head. But it missed me and wounded one of the prisoners. I had to tech him off. The rest surrendered without any more trouble.

However, this left York with a little problem: he was isolated behind enemy lines, in charge of dozens of German prisoners, there were several wounded American soldiers to consider, he had only himself and seven remaining able-bodied American doughboys as resources . . . and he was now the ranking man still in one piece!

> So we had about 80 or 90 Germans there disarmed and had another line of Germans to go through to get out. So I called for my men and one of them answered from behind a big oak tree and the others were on my right in the brush so I said lets get these germans out of here. So one of my men said it is impossible so I said no lets get them out. So when my men said that this german major said how many have you got and I said I have got a plenty and pointed my pistol at him all the time—in this battle I was using a rifle or a 45 Colts automatic pistol. So I line the germans up in a line of twos and got between the ones in front and I had the german magor before me. So I marched them straight into those other machine guns and I got them . . . I ordered the prisoners to pick up and carry our

wounded. I wasn't a-goin' to leave any good American boys lying out there to die. So I made the Germans carry them. And they did. And I takened the major and placed him at the head of the column and I got behind him and used him as a screen. I poked the Colt in his back and told him to hike. And he hiked. I guess I had him bluffed.

The only way York was able to control the suspicious Vollmer was to convince him that the eight visible doughboys were merely part of a far larger group of American soldiers all around him. (Although one has to wonder if, after watching Alvin York in action, Vollmer would've wanted to take any chances with even the big Tennessean alone!) York had to decide in which direction to march the men. He asked Vollmer, who indicated a gully angling off behind them.

> It was pretty hard to tell in the brush and with all the noise and confusion around which way to go. The major done suggested we go down the gully. Then I knowed that was the wrong way. And I told him we were not going down any gully. We were going straight through the German front-line trenches back to the American lines. It was their second line that I had captured. We sure did get a long way behind the German trenches.
>
> And so I done marched them straight at that old German front-line trench. And some more machine gunners swung around to fire. I told the major to blow his whistle or I would take his head and theirs too. So he blowed his whistle and they all done surrendered. All except one. I made the major order him to surrender twice. But he wouldn't. And I had to tech him off. I hated to do it. I've been doing a tol'able lot of thinking about it since. He was probably a brave soldier boy. But I couldn't afford to take any chances, and so I had to let him have it. There was considerably over a hundred prisoners now . . .

Actually, there were now so many enemy soldiers amassed that York feared his group would be mistaken for a German attack as they approached American lines and bombarded with artillery! However, as they came down the slope of the hill, a command to halt rang out, and York found himself at the point of a half-dozen rifles wielded by another American patrol. Astounded by the story of what had transpired (and, no doubt, the 100-plus disarmed Germans fronting them), the American soldiers escorted York, his men, and their prisoners back to friendly lines.

York took his prisoners across the American lines and up to his battalion headquarters, and here he met with another problem. As he put it, "We had such a mess of German prisoners that nobody seemed to want to take them over. So he had to take them back a right-far piece ourselves." York marched his prisoners from his battalion headquarters to regimental headquarters at Chatel Chehery, and from there all the way to his division headquarters to finally turn them over to the military police. York said, "On the way back we were constantly under heavy shell fire and I had to double-time them to get them through safely. There was nothing to be gained by having any more of them wounded or killed. They done surrendered to me and it was up to me to look after them. And so I done done it. I had orders to report to Brigadier General Lindsay, our brigadier commander, and he said to me, 'Well, York, I hear you have captured the whole damned German army.' And I told him I only had 132."

York was so tortured by the idea that any American soldiers might have been left behind still alive that the next day he secured permission to take a detail back to the scene of the fight to search for survivors.

The world went wild when the story of York's exploits became known, once they got past the initial amazement. After all, the entire thing—going one-on-one with a German machine-gun nest and winning, the bayonet charge, capturing an entire battalion of German soldiers practically unaided—seemed more like a larger-than-life tall tale than anything that could actually be accomplished by a single human being. As York biographer Tom Skeyhill would write, years later, "At first I was skeptical. Who was not? It sounded too much like a fairy tale. It just could not be done. It was not human. Yet it was done. Therefore, it could be done and it was human." The events were verified beyond a shadow of a doubt. There were the affidavits of the surviving doughboys who were with York (and who, by their own admission, took almost no part in the actual battle). Military authorities checked these events up one side and down the other, and it was incontrovertible that, as superhuman as it seemed, this simple, devout, conscientious objector Tennessee "mountain man" had actually done it!

York's promotion to sergeant followed swiftly. He was awarded the Medal of Honor by a special act of Congress. He was also awarded the French Legion of Honour, the Croix de Guerre with palms, the Medaille Militaire, the Italian War Cross, and a number of other high Allied decorations. York was given so many medals he joked he'd have to wear two coats if he wanted to wear them all at the same time. New York City, the "hardest town in the world," went nuts over this sturdy, freckle-faced Tennessean with the flaming-red hair and threw him a parade on his return to the United States. He was offered fortunes to go into movies, on the stage, to write for the big newspaper syndicates, to sign advertisements, but he turned his back on all of that with the somewhat naive comment, "Wouldn't I look funny in tights?" and returned to the Tennessee hills. As he put it, "Jes lit out for the old log cabin in the mountains and the little old mother and them-there hound-dogs of mine and the life where I belong."

We might ask ourselves just why Alvin York became such a hero, especially in America. And York's deeds still strike a responsive chord in us to this day. (Even Audie Murphy, decades later, would not inspire the enduring adulation accorded York, although arguably Murphy's wartime feats were even more impressive.) Foremost, of course, is the fact that York's actions are, on the face of it, worthy of hero worship. But there are other, less obvious reasons. Writing in *Sergeant York: An American Hero* (another important source of information for this chapter), author David D. Lee theorizes that York's incredible feat of arms occurred at a time when America was still reeling from the economic and cultural changes brought about by the Industrial Revolution. Alvin York was a living embodiment of traditional American virtues, such as deep piety, individualism, personal skill at arms, intense family devotion, and a hardy pioneer spirit, which were even then fading away. The fact that York was able to go up against the machine gun (at that time the most feared weapon of the machine age) and *win* reinforced to the American people that the ideals he represented were still alive, still an important part of American culture, and superior to anything else in the world. That belief persists to this day. I find it fascinating that whenever Alvin York is mentioned, he is invariably referred to with pride as "an *American* hero." One acquaintance of mine commented, "I don't think there's any other country in the world that could've produced a man like Alvin York."

I must confess I started the research that eventually became this chapter simply out of a burning curiosity as to whether York had actually stopped that German bayonet charge with a .45, as fans of the 1911 auto insist with almost evangelical zeal. But by the time I was through, Alvin York had emerged as one of my personal heroes. Far from being a Ramboesque killer (numerous decades before Rambo even existed), York was a dedicated pacifist who hated war and killing . . . but he realized that there are some things worth fighting for, and if you've got to fight, you'd better do a damned good job of it. As York said in his memoirs:

> I didn't want to kill a whole heap of Germans nohow. I didn't hate them. But I done it jes the same. I had to. I was cornered. It was either them or me, and I'm a-telling you I didn't and don't want to die nohow if I can live. If they done surrendered as I wanted them to when I hollered to them first, and kept on hollering to them, I would have given them the protection that I give them later when I tuk them back. But they wouldn't surrender, and there was no way out for me but to tech them off.

York's 1928 "autobiography" begins with a dedication:

> TO OUR OWN LEAGUE OF NATIONS. The American-born boys and the Greeks, Irish, Poles, Jews, and Italians who were in my platoon in the World War. A heap of them couldn't speak or write the American language until they larned it in the Army. Over here in the training camps and behind the lines in France a right-smart lot of them boozed, gambled, cussed, and went AWOL. But once they got into it Over There they kept on a-going. They were only tol'able shots and burned up a most awful lot of ammunition. But jest the same they always kept on a-going. Most of

them died like men, with their rifles and bayonets in their hands and their faces to the enemy. I'm a-thinkin' they were real heroes. Any way they were my buddies. I jes learned to love them.

I like that. I like it a lot.

York once said of his home in the Tennessee mountains, "I like it here. I wouldn't ever like it anywhere else. . . . I was born here and I'll die here. No sir, they won't take me to Arlington. When I die they'll put me away with the rest of the folks in the old family graveyard."

Alvin York died on September 2, 1964. That most common of men and most unlikely of heroes is buried in a simple grave site in the Valley of the Three Forks of the Wolf River, Cumberland County, Tennessee.

CHAPTER FIVE

FIREPOWER vs. THE "ONE-SHOT STOP"

If you have an important point to make, don't try to be subtle or clever. Use a pile driver. Hit the point once. Then come back and hit it again. Then hit it a third time—a tremendous whack.
— Sir Winston Spencer Churchill

There are basically two schools of thought on the topic of the high-capacity auto pistol. School #1 states that, in the middle of a real fight, it's absolutely amazing how fast you can run out of ammo. In all probability, the ammunition that's on your person when the balloon goes up is all you're gonna have to run with, so it's a very good thing to ensure that "how much ammo I've got on me" consists of quite a few rounds, both in spare magazines *and* initial in-gun capacity. School #2 says a high-cap handgun is a crutch for crappy marksmanship, that a high magazine capacity encourages shooters to spray ammo all over the countryside instead of focusing on the fundamentals of marksmanship. Salvation, however, is found in shot placement, and so you are far better off with a "low-cap" weapon capable of spewing out a few high-powered manstoppers, backed up by the skill to put them where they'll do the most good. Two nice theories, right? Let's discuss just how well both these arguments hold up in the real world.

In 1989, Dick Fairburn, a prolific police writer, conducted a survey through the pages of *Police Marksman* magazine. In a unique approach to gathering data on real-world shootings, this publication ran a one-page questionnaire in numerous issues of the magazine for police officers to respond to on the results of shooting incidents. Four years later, after the data from 241 shootings submitted was tabulated, the results of the survey were published in the March/April 1993 issue of *Police Marksman*. (The Fairburn/*Police Marksman* tests are reported on at length in Chapter 6 of Marshall and Sanow's book *Street Stoppers*).

The survey began with this question and statement: "Which ammunition has the best stopping power? The purpose of the PMA/Fairburn study is to gather factual data on the stopping power of various ammunition. This is a five-year study. We will only accept reports from police, military police, and trained security officers. Please submit the report in a departmental envelope with some detachable evidence that you are a law enforcement officer (business card). This evidence will be removed as soon as it is received. It is for verification purposes only. Report on an incident that was personally witnessed. Please be as accurate as possible. Only accurate facts derived from these forms can yield the scientifically valid results we are seeking."

This approach to information gathering may be criticized, of course, on the grounds that all the data accumulated depended on the honesty and objectivity of the respondents, whether eyewitnesses or the officers actually involved in the shootings. Also, to a certain extent we're dealing with subjective impressions here. And since all respondents to the survey were guaranteed anonymity, the details of these shootings could not be verified by independent sources. (This is a criticism that has long been leveled at Evan Marshall's findings, as well . . . by Dick Fairburn, among others!) Be that as it may, Fairburn deserves praise because, unlike many in this polarized debate, he did not develop a theory and defend it against all comers. Instead, as Evan Marshall had done before him, Fairburn went to the street to see what was happening in the real world. Although hardly definitive, the results of this survey do raise some interesting points on the topic of defensive handgun ammunition stopping power and handgun capacity.

The readers of *Police Marksman* submitted the results of 241 shootings in which 876 shots were fired. The range of calibers ran the gamut from .22 Long Rifle to .44 Magnum in handguns, and also included incidents with centerfire rifles and 12-gauge shotguns.

Differences in methodology between the Fairburn and Marshall studies are numerous. For instance, Fairburn focused on only four handgun calibers: the .38 Special, .357 Magnum, 9mm Parabellum, and .45 ACP. The .40 S&W and 10mm Auto were not included in the study. Fairburn, limiting himself to these four calibers, based his findings on 187 shootings in which 700 shots were fired. Right away we see a cherished icon bite the bullet (pun intended), the ideal of the "one-shot stop." As we can see from these results, in the real world anything you can fire out of a handgun is going to be, in the overall scheme of things, so underpowered that it is often necessary to fire far more than a single hit to definitively stop a determined assailant.

Also, Marshall restricts his results to those shootings in which only one torso hit was fired, which I feel tends to artificially inflate the final percentages. In Marshall's findings, the shootings where a single shot to the chest is fired and the bad guy drops get counted; the incidents where it is necessary to shoot someone more than once do not. In the real world, when you shoot someone once and he keeps right on trying to kill you, what do you do? Instantly shoot him again, of course! And as soon as you do that, the shooting gets factored right out of Marshall's stats, "to remove as many variables as possible." When all you're counting is one-hit gunfights and ignoring anything else, is it any wonder that one-shot stops seem to happen an inordinate amount of time? All Marshall's statistics really ly tell us is the ratio of "one-shot stops" versus the number of "one-shot no-stops," and shootings where the bad guy gets shot once, doesn't stop, but is not shot again are comparatively rare. Fairburn, however, was interested only in how often a particular caliber worked, period. So he counted extremity hits, head shots, and shootings in which multiple bullet impacts were registered, which strikes me as being much more "real world." As you'll see in a moment, the stopping power percentages arrived at by Fairburn are far lower than those quoted by Marshall and, I feel, more in line with the sort of performance you can realistically expect from a handgun.

The first thing Fairburn wanted to determine was overall success ratio by caliber. Let's take a look at Fairburn's and Marshall's findings. For purposes of this comparison, I've refined Marshall's stats, which are normally broken down by load, into an overall average by caliber; this takes into account the performance of every load for which Marshall has numbers in all four calibers.

FAIRBURN OVERALL SUCCESSES

.45 ACP	54.5 percent
.357 Magnum	53.8 percent
9mm Parabellum	49.0 percent
.38 Special	39.0 percent

MARSHALL ONE-SHOT STOPS

.357 Magnum	90.8 percent
9mm Parabellum	79.7 percent
.45 ACP	75.7 percent
.38 Special	65.6 percent

The major difference between Fairburn's findings and Marshall's (aside from the fact the Marshall numbers would lead you to believe that handguns are much more powerful than is actually the case) is in the groupings of the calibers. Fairburn groups these four calibers into basically two levels of effectiveness, with the .357, 9mm, and .45 all showing a similar degree of performance and the .38 being considerably less effective. Marshall, on the other hand, breaks it down into three groups, with the 9mm and .45 being about the same, the .357 coming out as considerably better, and the .38 again at the bottom. We must acknowledge that Marshall's finding are based on far more shootings than the Fairburn survey (7,020 reports versus 187) and the overall results were tabulated using a far different set of criteria. Still, this is all fascinating food for thought, isn't it?

Fairburn did break the results of his shootings down by load, although, unlike Marshall, he groups all like types of ammo together. For instance, all 158-grain LSWC-HP +P "FBI Loads" went into a single category of performance, regardless of manufacturer. And in 9mm, all the 115-grain JHPs were broken down into two categories, Silvertip and non-Silvertip. However, those results are outside the scope of this chapter and so, other than to acknowledge their existence, will not be addressed here.

What *is* extremely relevant to the topic under discussion are two more pieces of data drawn from the Fairburn survey: the average number of shots fired per incident and the hit ratio per caliber. Ah, now we're getting to it! It has long been held (primarily by devotees of the SA Model of 1911, with its single-stack "low capacity" magazine) that having a gun that puts a lot of rounds at your fingertips induces in many shooters a tendency to "spray and pray" in a defensive emergency, i.e., point the gun in the general direction of the problem and hose down the area, hoping a lucky hit will compensate for a total lack of focus on marksmanship fundamentals.

Fairburn took the average number of rounds fired in all the gunfights that were reported to him and broke them down by caliber. The results are as follows:

CALIBER	SHOTS PER INCIDENT
9mm Parabellum	5.5 rounds
.38 Special	3.6 rounds
.45 ACP	2.7 rounds
.357 Magnum	2.3 rounds

On the surface, this would seem to corroborate the views of the spray-and-pray critics since those shooters armed with 9mm pistols fired far more rounds than those with any other weapon type. Several conclusions might be drawn from this: (1) Shooters armed with 9mms tend to hose the bad guy, and thus fire more rounds than shooters armed with lower capacity weapons. Those folks who hate the 9mm cartridge with a passion (again, primarily SA .45 shooters) might also instantly jump to conclusion (2): "See! You gotta shoot someone *twice* as many times to put 'em down with a 9mm as you do with a .45!"

Personally, I feel it may be argued with equal or greater logic that what we have here might more likely be an indicator of a particular weapon type's controllability. I'm not talking about whether you can fire hits, but just how *fast* and *easily* you may fire hits. In other words, as the weapon becomes more controllable, you are able to fire more rounds before the bad guy hits the ground. Look at Fairburn's stats in this area and it makes sense. The hardest type of weapon to shoot of all those ranked is the .357 Magnum revolver, combining as it does heavy recoil with a less than totally user-friendly (from the standpoint of "shootability") DA revolver mechanism. The second hardest gun to fire effectively in semitrained hands (and that's what you're talking about for most police officers) would be the .45 auto. In this weapon you've got a more user-friendly semiauto firing platform; however, this is offset to a large degree by recoil heavy enough to be a significant problem for the average cop. Moving right along, the light recoil of the .38 Special revolver makes it easier to fire than either of the prior two weapons, even given its long, heavy DA trigger pulls. Finally, the easiest weapon to fire fast and well would be the 9mm auto, combining as it does light recoil with the more "shootable" semiauto mechanism. Most gunfights are close-range, fast-paced affairs that are over in seconds. Is it any wonder that, all else being equal, you can light someone up with more rounds out of an auto pistol firing mild kickin' 9mms than with a DA revolver firing heavily recoiling .357 Magnums?

However, we still have to take into account the last of Fairburn's findings, that of hit ratio. What we see is as follows:

CALIBER	HIT RATIO
.357 Magnum	78.2 percent
.45 ACP	61.5 percent
.38 Special	57.3 percent
9mm Parabellum	47.3 percent

Well, that would certainly seem to support the spray-and-pray theory, wouldn't it? Not only do shooters armed with 9mms fire more rounds than those folks armed with other weapons, they also fire more *misses*. Now, this is not to say there is anything innately evil about a high-capacity handgun. However, it is an undeniable fact that for a certain type of individual (primarily one who went to the high-cap gun in a conscious attempt to compensate for inferior marksmanship skills) a high-capacity handgun does indeed become a self-fulfilling prophecy. This is extremely bad, as every miss is a wild shot that potentially endangers the lives of innocent bystanders. I've said it before and I'll say it again: the only safe resting place for bullets fired in self-defense is inside the body of the criminal who forced you to shoot in the first place!

Consider Fairburn's comments on the 9mm's performance in his findings: "The hits per shots ratio of 47.3 percent for the 9mm is the lowest shown. When the two aspects are combined (shots per incident and hit ratio), it can be said that the high-capacity, semiauto pistols need some careful attention paid to the aspects of marksmanship and fire control."

This data would seem to call into question the conventional wisdom that heavily recoiling handguns cannot be used well by the rank and file (which I just repeated myself not too long ago, you may have noticed). The heavy kickin' .45 ACP and .357 Magnum had higher hit ratios than the comparatively lightly recoiling 9mm and .38 Special. Taking this into account in conjunction with the number-of-rounds-fired-per-gunfight data, we might be tempted to conclude that while the 9mm and .38 Special may be fired faster, any of these calibers can be shot accurately enough to win a gunfight. This casts doubt on the theory that the heavy recoil of the .357 Magnum renders it a poor choice for self-defense for any but the most hardened pistoleros. As a matter of fact (as is pointed out in *Street Stoppers*), if we were to take Fairburn's findings as the last word on real-world handgun usage, we should probably all be carrying .357 Magnum revolvers!

Be that as it may, many shooters, even those with high skill levels, simply feel more comfortable with a gun that gives them double-digit mag capacity (just as some people don't feel adequately armed with any auto pistol that's not a .45, etc.). And more power to 'em, I say! You've got to go with what feels right to you. Provided the gun chosen is at least reasonably appropriate for the task at hand (and it's a weapon you can shoot well), I feel you're always better off choosing a gun you really like over the recommendations of any "expert" . . . including your 'umble servant here!

Most people I know who carry single-stack "low-capacity" autos carry only one spare magazine. And those folks armed with double-stack handguns generally carry *no* spare ammo. If you ask them why, they'll say something like, "Hey, the reason I went to a gun that holds this many rounds was so I don't have to carry spare ammo," or "If I can't do it with 16 shots, I figure that means I'm dead anyway." Personally, that last statement seems to me akin to programming yourself to die. I don't know about you, but whether my gunfight goes one round or 50, I plan to survive!

I think people's feelings about magazine capacity usually have a lot to do with what sort of gun they started out shooting (and/or carrying). To them, however much ammo that gun contained came to seem "normal," their baseline for comparison, and any deviation from that standard will have either positive or negative connotations. Take, for instance, the old cop who for years had to carry a six-shot revolver, but then was given permission to carry an eight-shot single-stack 1911. Since six shots has become for him the norm, having eight is a definite step up, and if he one day goes to a gun that holds 15, 16, or even 18 rounds . . . well, then he's got all the ammo in the world! For the shooter who started off with a 16-shot handgun, however, *that* is his baseline, and when he contemplates the prospect of carrying, say, the aforementioned eight-shot Colt .45, his attitude is, "My God . . . that's *half* the ammo!"

So, is it really necessary to have a high magazine capacity in your self-defense handgun? Arguably, no. Assuming your shots are hitting the mark, most self-defense shootings will be over before you can exhaust the ammo supply in a low-capacity weapon. The high-capacity handgun provides us with an ammo reservoir that will only ever be needed in the most extreme and unusual circumstances. However, it may also be argued that the possibility of extreme and unusual circumstances is the reason we carry handguns in the first place. And because most of us don't usually carry around our crystal balls with us, we're just not gonna know how many rounds we need in a gunfight until we find out through first-hand experience.

We also have to ask ourselves, is carrying a high-cap handgun an engraved invitation to the spray-and-pray syndrome? Again, arguably, no. I do think the attitude some people have, that anyone who carries a high-cap auto must be a hose artist who can't shoot accurately, is a bit bogus. What these people don't seem to realize is that both accuracy and fire control are determined by *the shooter, not the gun*. Just 'cause you're carryin' a high-cap auto doesn't mean you have to spray and pray, just as carrying a low-cap auto doesn't automatically make you a marvel of precision shooting. Although sprayin' and prayin' is primarily associated with high-capacity autoloaders, I can assure you it does indeed happen even among shooters armed with five-shot revolvers. And I've seen a lot of folks armed with the "ultimate shooting machine," the eight-shot Colt .45 auto, who are mediocre pistoleros at best, as well as many people totin' around high-cap guns who are deadly fast and accurate. (The vice, of course, is also versa.)

Given my personal set of priorities, I find that how a particular weapon fits my hand and how swiftly and well it may be brought into play to deliver rapid-fire center hits on a man-sized target at close combat range are of far more importance to me than its magazine capacity. Now, it just so happens the handgun that, for my personal use, provides the best combination of hand-to-grip fit and "pointability," coupled with great reliability and "shootability," is the Glock 19, a compact high-capacity 9mm. While the high mag capacity is not why I chose this gun, as long as it's there anyway, I certainly can't consider that a bad thing!

In a real-world defensive emergency, almost any decent, 100-percent reliable handgun can save the day. Of course, any of them can also fail. Success or lack thereof will depend primarily upon the skill and courage of the weapon's user, and will (probably) have very little or nothing to do with the specifics of the gun's caliber, action type . . . or capacity. This is only my personal opinion, but the shootings I've examined have left me with the feeling you can probably make a good case for the defensive handgun containing about a dozen cartridges. If you need more than that, you're probably just not hitting the target, and so having more ammo available is kind of like throwing good money after bad. It's not who fires the first shot or the most shots, but who fires the *last* shot that counts.

Now, all that does not mean I'm going to stop carrying my 16-shot Glock 19 or the two spare magazines with which I regularly back it up. Firearms instructor Greg Hamilton of InSights Training Center, like myself, also carries a Glock 19, but with only one spare magazine versus my two. (The main difference between us, of course, is that Greg fires his gun just a whole lot better than I do mine.) Greg likes to look at my double-mag pouch and ask, "Duane, what are you going to *do* with all that ammo?" My answer: "Hopefully . . . nothing!" When it comes to my ammunition supply, like the old saying goes, I'd rather have it and not need it than need it and not have it. I have enough faith in my training to possess a reasonable certainty that any bullets loosed by myself in combat will go where they need to go and not wind up instead perforating things like walls, furniture, and other incidentals, including the occasional innocent bystander. If that is the case, if your high-cap handgun is coupled with the ability to fire it fast and accurately, then I regard having lots of rounds on tap not as a necessity, not as the compensation for lousy shooting skills it is commonly perceived to be, but as more of a luxury. And if you *can* carry a couple of spare magazines for your high-cap autoloader, comfortably and concealed . . . well, why not? It's not like it's costing you anything!

The police firearms instructors to whom I've talked all tell me that the hardest gun-handling skill for shooters to execute under the stress of a real fight is reloading, with either a revolver or auto. Reloading a handgun is a fine motor skill, requiring us to move both hands with precision relative to each other. Unfortunately, our fine motor skill is one of the first things to go under the adrenaline dump of the fight-or-flight syndrome. This is a problem that can be, to a large extent, overcome by diligent training. However, the sad truth is that very few people who carry a gun on a daily basis, in either the police or civilian sectors, have committed themselves to that level of training. So, basically, the average shooter can count on the ammo that's already in the gun as being easily available, but when that runs dry he hits a major snag in the proceedings. That being the case, would it not make sense to carry guns that allow us to put off the moment when our slides lock back and we absolutely *have* to reload as long as possible? (And before I get 10 letters pointing it out, yes, I know that in a perfect world we'd always reload before our guns went dry. Anyone out there live in a perfect world?)

So, looking back over this chapter, what have we deduced about the high-capacity autoloader? Well, we know this a system that can be abused . . . but then again, it doesn't have to be! And you probably won't need all those rounds . . . but on the other hand, you just might! My God, that does seem wishy-washy, doesn't it? A good case may be made both for and against these guns.

When it comes time to defend your life, even a bottomless magazine loaded with an infinite number of cartridges will not save you unless it's coupled with serious attention to the basics of marksmanship. Only hits count! All a high-capacity autoloader provides is a system that allows you to keep on delivering those hits in "extreme circumstances" longer between reloads than any other kind of sidearm.

You know, it always struck me, in the dear, dead days when the most burning controversy within the handgunning fraternity was "Which is best, the .45 or 9mm?" that it really came down to a question of what most scared the person making the decision: if the idea of shooting someone and having them not stop scared you more, then you chose a .45; if it was the concept of dying with an empty gun in your hands that started up the cold sweats, you chose a high-capacity 9mm. Simple.

I do think, however, that both those decision-making processes are flawed. To the people who chose a .45 because of it's theoretically superior "stopping power" I have this to say: if you honestly believe any realistic defensive handgun will give you reliable manstopping power, you're living in a fantasy world. Meanwhile, back in reality, there's simply no way to pack any appreciable level of power into something as tiny as a handgun cartridge.

Similarly, it's always seemed to me that the people who just had to have a high-capacity handgun evinced a basic lack of faith in their own marksmanship. Of these two approaches, I do tend to feel that those folks who believe there might possibly be some advantage to having a lot of rounds in-gun have a more defensible position than those who believe in fairies, um, I mean handgun stopping power. Still, I've seen some pretty bizarre manifestations of the high-capacity fetish.

I remember an incident that occurred when I was attending a local pistol match at which most of the shooters were police officers. In the clubhouse after the match I overheard an absolutely fascinating conversation between two shooters, one of whom was a Tacoma cop armed with a high-capacity Beretta 92, the other a civilian packin' a Colt Government Model .45 backed up by two single-stack magazines in a spare mag pouch. The cop began to explain (lecture?) to the Government Model-equipped shooter on how, considering the incredibly dangerous job he was called upon to do, he had to have a high-capacity auto as a duty weapon (in his case the aforementioned Beretta 9mm with 16 rounds in the gun and two spare 15-round mags on his duty belt) "to deal with all the gang violence."

Now, let me tell you something, folks: we do have gangbangers here in that pearl of the Pacific Northwest—Tacoma, Washington— but the problem is really not that bad. Oh, the media likes to play it up as being a lot worse than it is (more dramatic on the evening news, don't you know), but the Tacoma gangs are extremely localized in one small neighborhood, and even then they're not all they're cracked up to be. Tacoma's Hilltop area ain't exactly South Central L.A., sports fans. So I did feel our police orator might be overdramatizing the danger level to which he was exposed . . . just a tad!

Continuing on, he said, "Why, just last week I put a guy up against the car, and when I frisked him I reached inside his jacket and pulled out an MP5!" Listening in on this, the thought skittered through my mind, "Let's see, an MP5 is about as big as a super-extra-large, economy-sized box of Cheerios, and it weighs about 10 pounds. Whew! That guy's jacket must've had *some* pockets!" The speaker's partner, who was also attending the match (and who seemed comparatively intelligent), looked incredibly embarrassed at his partner's antics and muttered, "Actually, it was a Tec-9." Now, that's still a big gun to carry stuffed inside your jacket, but at least it's believable!

And here we come to the most absurd of all the ridiculous statements I heard our high-cap Beretta shooter make that day: "What if I get jumped by 12 guys, and all I've got is your eight-shot .45? I mean, you know things are getting crazy when you reach into a guy's jacket and you pull out an MP5!" (This was just a short few days after the L.A. riots, and what you'd do if you were caught in the middle of a mob was, I assume, on the minds of anyone who regularly carries a handgun.) From his partner came the repeated mutter, "Actually, it was a Tec-9."

Now, allow me to digress for a moment while I discuss this whole "riot" thing, since that is one of the common arguments put forth by high-cap auto fans. A few months before the incident I'm recounting, Jan Libourel, editor of Petersen's *Handguns* magazine, had done one of his famous "Ask the Experts" articles (where he poses a particular query to a variety of gun experts and then publishes their responses) in which the question went something like this: "You're going overseas. You'll be staying an extended period of time. It will be legal for you to take with you one handgun. It will also be legal for you to carry it concealed. You can take with you as much ammunition as necessary to fulfill your needs on the trip, and spare parts and pistolsmithing services will be available for whatever gun you choose." (This last bit was inserted, I'm sure, to avoid hopelessly prejudicing things in favor of the 9mm, which is the most popular service-gun chambering outside the United States, and the Browning Hi-Power, which is by far the most popular heavy-duty handgun in foreign countries that allow their citizens to own weapons in military calibers.) "You may need this gun to hunt game. You may need it for concealed carry and personal defense." And here we come to the biggie: "Riots are a possibility, and this will be your only weapon should you be caught up in one."

Now, the interesting thing is that all of the respondents who really worried about the "riot possibility" part of the question—and *who had never actually been in a riot*—considered high magazine capacity a major plus. The only respondent who had any real-world experience with riots was associate editor Dave Arnold during his days in Rhodesian law enforcement, and Dave's choice was a six-shot .357 Magnum revolver! As near as I can remember the quote, Dave said, "In my experience, rioters always break and run as soon as you fire the first few shots . . . and if they don't, you'll be ripped to pieces before all those rounds in your high-capacity magazine could do you any good, anyway." I read those words and thought to myself, "Wow . . . reality." I found this hard-headed, extremely realistic, no-BS attitude quite impressive.

Now, back to our hero cop and his "I've-gotta-have-a-high-capacity-gun-because-I'm-in-such-danger-what-if-I-get-caught-in-a-riot" attitude. Our .45 shooter looked at him and said, "You know, you could've taken me, my eight-shot .45 and two spare magazines, and dropped me right down in the middle of the worst rioting in L.A., and I guarantee you I would've walked out of there. There's something you don't understand that I do, and that's why people riot."

"Oh, yeah? Why do people riot?"

"Well, the first thing you can forget is that 'protesting against social injustice' BS. People riot because it's *fun*. Think about it: you get to run around and scream at the top of your lungs, and that's fun . . . it's a great way to relieve stress! You get to break windows and set things on fire, and that's fun. Maybe you pick yourself up a free color television set, occasionally you beat some guy to death . . . and that's fun, too. But you know what's not fun? *Dying* is not fun; being shot to death is not fun. And when the mob came for me and I blew the brains of the first couple of guys all over the faces of everyone around them, I guarantee you the rest of them would go find somewhere else to play . . . and if they didn't, I'd be ripped apart before all the rounds in a high-capacity magazine could do me any good, anyway." (I've always wondered if this fellow had also read that great Dave Arnold quote a few months before.)

Mister 9mm looked at Mister .45 with this pitying, superior expression on his face, and sadly shook his head. "That's *old* thinking, man." Apparently, the "old thinking" to which he referred is the idea that if you hit what you're aiming at, you don't need a high-capacity handgun.

Actually, I felt that both those guys had points. But if they wear hats maybe they'll be able to hide them!

CHAPTER SIX

ARE REVOLVERS OBSOLETE?

It's just six of one and half-a-dozen of the other.
—Frederick Marryat
The Pirate

The last few decades of the 20th century have seen a tremendous transition away from the DA revolver and toward the auto pistol in police service. At the same time, this trend has been mirrored by the actions of armed civilians who purchase autos over revolvers for their home defense/concealed carry guns. Articles in gun magazines sporting titles like "Is the Revolver Dead?" have become commonplace. Well, I hate to be the one to say it, but really . . . the answer is YES! It *is* rather hard to make a case for the DA revolver as being anything but an adequate (but by no means excellent, by modern standards) fighting sidearm.

Still, there are those who recommend the revolver as a superior choice in a defensive handgun, largely by virtue of its greater simplicity of operation and (supposedly) higher reliability rate versus an auto. Where the autoloader is alleged to be much more unreliable than the revolver, the wheelgun is held up as a paragon of functional dependability. In reality, this is hardly the truth. A good case can be made for the revolver's great reliability being primarily a myth and for this basic gun design possessing flaws and functional problems that make it far from the best choice around when it comes time to choose a serious combat handgun.

Although I do feel that, in general, you *may* get a higher level of reliability from a generic out-of-the-box revolver than an equivalent auto pistol, there are many things that revolvers simply do not do well. In this chapter, I will not be reviewing the tired old "revolver versus auto" argument. Rather, I'll be evaluating the shortcomings of the revolver on its own merits, with no reference to autos at all (save where there is really no way to avoid the truth that auto pistols perform so much better than revolvers in a particular area we simply must acknowledge the fact). Now, let us consider first what revolvers don't do well.

WHAT REVOLVERS DON'T DO WELL

Clearing Malfunctions

Although revolvers may indeed, on average, malfunction less often than autos, when they do choke they're one helluva lot harder to get up and running again.

Firearms experts make an important distinction between the two types of weapon malfunctions: stoppages and jams. A stoppage is a minor malfunction that can be swiftly and easily cleared by the shooter himself, in seconds, using only his hands. Most auto pistol malfunctions are stoppages, not jams. A jam, on the other hand, is a major malfunction that ties the gun up so tight there's no way the shooter can swiftly restore it to a functional state. Unfortunately, most revolver malfunctions are jams. Grains of powder or brass shavings in one or more of a revolver's chambers, a high primer, or an over-long cartridge all can create a condition of insufficient headspace that'll bind a revolver's cylinder so badly it'll take a few whacks with a rubber mallet just to open the action.

One of the most common revolver malfunctions, a shell casing stuck under the extractor star, is a jam, requiring tools (and time) to clear. The usual cause of this jam is that the shooter hasn't opened the action all the way when punching out the empties. Thus, as the extractor star begins to extract the empty shells, the base of the inwardmost cartridge casing catches on the side of the recoil shield, forcing the extractor star up and over its rim. Oversized target grips also can sometimes catch a casing in such a fashion. When this happens, the extractor star is blocked from returning to its normal position, which prevents the cylinder from being reloaded and the action from being closed.

The really bad news is that the extractor star is now on *top* of the spent casing, blocking it from being pulled out of the cylinder. Clearing this jam requires holding the extractor star in its rearmost position via pressure on the ejector rod, inserting a dowel or something similar into the chamber to push the casing as far out as possible, then plucking it out of the gun with your fingers. Some revolver armed shooters carry a "dejamming" rod with them, on the theory that they'll use it to clear out the gun should this problem occur in the middle of a gunfight. In my opinion, they're kidding themselves. If your gun ever chokes this severely at the "moment of truth" you might as well just throw it away and either go to Gun #2 or run like hell! You would, in overwhelming probability, be dead before you could complete the complicated and time-consuming remedial action for this particular jam.

Surviving Abuse

The swing-out cylinder DA revolver is, by its very nature, a somewhat fragile and finely fitted instrument. While the revolver handles *neglect* better than an auto, it is far less able to survive *abuse*, which is the primary reason autoloaders were adopted by most of world's armies early in this century. The alignment of the weapon's cylinder, crane, yoke, and ejector rod must be perfect or the action will bind up. A blow to the gun that probably wouldn't faze an auto, such as accidentally dropping it on a hard surface, could easily spring a revolver's cylinder in the crane, rendering it unserviceable. Armed good guys have had occasion to use their handguns as field-expedient bludgeons over the years, and revolvers are notorious for breaking under such treatment.

"Shooting Dirty"

An auto can be fired for many more rounds than a revolver before fouling interferes with normal functioning. Simply put, shoot a revolver for long without cleaning and it will malfunction or stop working entirely far sooner than a comparable quality auto pistol. When fouling begins to accumulate inside the finely fitted revolver mechanism, tolerances swiftly plunge below operational levels. For instance, powder buildup on the front of the cylinder and the forcing cone will cause the two pieces to drag against each other, interfering with cylinder rotation. Grains of powder in the crane/yoke area can prevent the action from being closed. Fouling in the chambers can prevent rounds from fully chambering, creating a condition of insufficient headspace that will not allow the weapon's cylinder to rotate.

The area in which revolver performance is most swiftly eroded by fouling is in how fast you can reload the gun. Get a bit of crud in a revolver's chambers and, when using speedloaders, the cartridges won't fall smoothly into place through force of gravity alone. Usually, you'll wind up with one or two cartridges still protruding partially from the chambers; you then have to complete the insertion by hand, shoving the recalcitrant rounds into place. Use poor reloading technique, and it's quite possible your gun will begin to screw up this way the very first time you go to recharge it! It is very important when reloading a revolver to hold the gun straight up and down while you punch out the empties; this allows unburned flakes of powder to fall free from the chambers during the reloading process.

Whenever I go to handgun training classes where hundreds of rounds are fired every day, the folks shooting revolvers have to frequently come off the line to brush out their guns. Autos are far more tolerant of this sort of abuse. At one shooting class I attended, I put more than 800 rounds through a Browning Hi-Power in one day without cleaning it and without a single malfunction. I've also put more than 1,000 rounds through my SIG P228 in a day, also without cleaning or problems. There's not a revolver on earth that could do the same thing.

Reloading Ease and Speed

The police firearms instructors to whom I've talked all tell me that reloading, whether a revolver or auto pistol (but especially the revolver), is the single hardest skill for a shooter to execute under the stress of a real fight. One of the first things to go under the adrenaline dump of the fight-or-flight reflex is your fine motor control, and reloading a revolver *is* a high-dexterity operation. Here is one case where I simply must compare the auto to the revolver: fitting a single large magazine into an auto's mag well is far more easily accomplished than simultaneously aligning multiple rounds with the corresponding chambers in a revolver's cylinder.

Also consider that with an auto, it's a simple matter to carry your spare magazines on the off-side hip and grab the spare ammo with your non-gun hand as the strong hand thumb punches out the mag in the gun. With the revolver, in order to have any chance of completing the reloading operation smoothly, you need to switch the gun to your weak hand and insert the spare ammo with your more dexterous dominant hand. This causes a couple of problems. For one, it greatly complicates and slows the reloading technique. For another, if you carry your spare revolver ammo on the off-side hip, it's almost impossible to get to with your strong-side hand when you need it. Putting the speedloaders on the same side as the gun is impractical from the standpoint of comfort and concealment. Some shoulder holsters have provisions for spare ammo to be carried on the side opposite the gun, which is a minor improvement, but most people who carry a revolver have got a speedloader or two rattling around somewhere in the bottom of a jacket pocket, where it will be extremely slow to access, or they carry their ammo in the less bulky speedstrips (if the gun is a .38 or .357—speedstrips only come in one size).

And yes, I do realize that revolver maestro Jerry Miculek carries his Safariland Comp-III speedloaders on his off-hand side, just like spare auto pistol magazines, and when he reloads he leaves the gun in his right hand, using the left to insert the speedloader; Miculek can reload a wheelgun faster that most people can recharge an autoloader. It is also true that Jerry Miculek is (a) functionally ambidextrous and (b) the best in the world at what he does. For us mere mortals, the auto pistol has a huge advantage when it comes time to reload. Which brings us to carrying spare ammo.

Carrying Spare Ammo

One of the reasons autos have been become so much more popular than revolvers as serious carry guns lately is that the shape of the spare ammo carriers favors the auto. Flat, slim pistol magazines lend themselves to easy, comfortable carry in a spare mag pouch, but revolver speedloaders must of necessity be every bit as big around as the weapon's cylinder, so packing the spare ammo is almost as big a pain in the butt as carrying the gun itself.

Revolver speedstrips are considerably easier to tote (which is why so many people who carry wheelguns carry their spare ammo in compact speedstrips instead of bulky speedloaders). Unfortunately, speedstrips are, all else being equal, considerably slower and more fumble prone during a reload than speedloaders. I do find, however, that although the necessary process of inserting rounds into the cylinder one or two at a time with speedstrips makes them technically slower than speedloaders, the fact that speedstrips can be carried accessibly in a jeans watch pocket or belt pouch versus groping around in a pocket for a speedloader saves you enough time to more than offset the speedstrips' slower reloading speed.

Capacity

This is perhaps the most commonly touted advantage of auto pistols over revolvers. Traditional ammunition capacity of a medium- or large-framed revolver is six rounds, although the very smallest snubbies hold five. Of late, we've seen Smith & Wesson introduce a seven-shot .357 Magnum L-frame, and Taurus has chambered its large-framed revolver design for first seven, then eight shots of .357. Still, I have to view these attempts to improve the revolver's "firepower" with something of a jaundiced eye. A high-capacity revolver is a serious oxymoron! High capacity is the auto pistol's forte, not the revolver's. Basically, these guns are an attempt to compete with the auto at its own game, and that's a sucker move. To increase a service revolver's capacity beyond six rounds, you have to go to a gun that is much wider and heavier than an auto holding far more ammo. Which leads us to comfortable carry.

Comfortable Carry

The biggest problem I have with revolvers as carry guns is not their limited ammunition capacity, not the fact that they're harder to shoot than some autos (more about this in a moment), nor the slow, dexterity-dependent reloading sequence. It is, rather, the fact that a revolver chambered for a serious combat caliber is a large, heavy beast that is considerably less comfortable to carry and conceal than an equivalent auto pistol. I mean, a Glock 19 fully loaded with 16 rounds weighs *less* than an *unloaded* six-shot 3-inch barreled Smith & Wesson K-frame! (Of course, the 1994 Crime Bill, with its fatuous prohibition on future manufacture and importation of auto pistol magazines holding more than 10 rounds, is supposedly the Great Equalizer that somewhat levels the playing field. Considering the literally millions of high-capacity magazines already in-country, I find that a bit hard to swallow. Everyone I know who really wants high-capacity magazines for their autos has them.)

Also against the revolver as a concealment weapon is its shape, which makes it far less comfortable to carry. Where the flat autoloader lies comfortably against the body, the revolver's rounded, protuberant cylinder tends to dig painfully into its carrier's side. Some folks say revolvers are harder than autos to conceal. I disagree: the hardest part of a gun to hide is the butt, and because the butt on almost all autos must of necessity be large enough to contain its magazine, handles on autoloaders are nearly always considerably larger than the grips on equivalent revolvers. Purely from a concealment standpoint, revolvers are easier to hide than autos; what they also are is considerably harder to conceal *comfortably*.

Recently, we've seen the introduction of truly small snub-nosed revolvers chambered for .357 Magnum, a trend I view with some alarm. Think about it: if it is the case that the medium-framed Smith & Wesson K-frame is far too light to weather a steady diet of full-power Magnums (and I assure you, it *is* the case), then how are these tiny pocket guns going to stand up? I'm aware of a case where a gunwriter was doing a review of one of these mini-Magnums. In the course of evaluating it, several hundred rounds were fired. The gun broke and needed repair three times!

Ease of Shooting

As any but the veriest tyro knows, SA autoloaders of Colt 1911, Browning Hi-Power, or Glock persuasion, et al, are far easier to fire fast and well than a revolver. It is simply much easier to hold a gun steady on target while applying four or five pounds of pressure over a fraction of an inch with such autos than to do the same thing while applying approximately two and a half or three times the poundage over most of an inch with a revolver.

It is true that some autoloader designs, like the conventional DA autos that switch from DA to SA between the first and second shots, are harder to master than revolvers. It is also true that revolvers can be shot well (very well, in trained hands); however, doing so is far more a matter of rhythm, timing, and fine motor control than with many autos. And remember, your fine motor control is cataclysmically impacted under the fight-or-flight reflex. Simply put, if you want a gun that is easy to shoot under the stress of a defensive emergency, there are designs out there that are far, *far* more forgiving than a DA revolver.

Novice shooters are often guided toward a DA revolver as their best choice in a defense gun because of its simple operating drill: point gun, pull trigger, repeat as necessary. However, I'm getting away from giving out that recommendation myself, especially to women. Many women, with their generally weaker hands, have trouble even pulling the trigger on a DA revolver, much less firing the piece fast and well.

SUMMARY

I don't want the foregoing to be seen as a blanket condemnation of the revolver as a defensive tool, either for law enforcement or civilian self-protection. The old wheelgun does have its positive attributes. These include safety and simplicity of operation in the usual untrained or semitrained hands, low maintenance, a nice size-to-power ratio in Magnum calibers, the existence of lightweight and extremely compact .38 snubbies (which may well be the best truly small handguns around), compatibility with pocket carry, and the fact that revolvers in general cost less than equivalent quality autos—if you elect to go the cheap route, then a cheap revolver *should* be more reliable than a cheap auto. For arming less-well-trained persons, the more idiotproof revolver would be the way to go (assuming our idiot has hands strong enough to pull the trigger, that is).

Still, it would be a mistake, I think, not to realize that the DA revolver is in many ways an antiquated device, mechanically fragile and lacking in cartridge capacity and robustness. In service-gun configuration these guns are heavy for the amount of ammo they hold and uncomfortable to carry concealed. Revolvers are slow and complicated to reload and not nearly as reliable as is commonly assumed. Really, the only revolvers for which a good case can be made, in my opinion, are the tiny .38 snubbies (since it *is* possible to make a revolver smaller than an equivalently powerful auto) and the big Magnums (since it's also possible to make a Magnum revolver more compact than a Magnum auto). For anything in between those two extremes of size, weight, and power (i.e., the sorts of guns serious people actually carry on a daily basis), it's just awfully hard to make a case for the revolver over a good combat autoloader.

C H A P T E R   S E V E N

JUST HOW GOOD IS THE .40 S&W?

Things are seldom what they seem.
Skim milk masquerades as cream.

—William Schwenck Gilbert
H.M.S. Pinafore

In the few short years since its introduction, the .40 Smith & Wesson cartridge has become a very popular defensive handgun chambering. The "Big Three" of combat auto pistol calibers would be the 9mm Parabellum, .40 S&W, and .45 ACP. The initial idea behind the .40 S&W was to give you (theoretically, at least) more stopping power than a 9mm and more magazine capacity than a .45. A lot of shooters like that idea: "Big bullets and lots of 'em" is kind of like a mantra with some people. (We're assuming, of course, that our .40 will be running pre-Crime Bill, full-capacity magazines to maximize that capacity advantage.) There *are* high-capacity .45s; however, the butts on these things are huge, as are the guns themselves. Also, the .45 ACP requires a large-framed sidearm, but the .40 can be and is chambered in medium-framed guns exactly the same size as the 9mm. Still, the more I've learned about the .40 S&W cartridge, the more I've come to doubt that it's really all that great an idea.

To start with, as I've studied just how the .40 S&W cartridge performs in handguns, I've come to the conclusion it should be chambered in large-framed guns only. The standard .40 S&W loading, 180 grains at approximately 980 fps, has very nearly the same level of recoil as a standard pressure 185-grain .45 JHP, which runs 950 fps or thereabouts. If you're going to have .45 ACP-level recoil, then it's going to take a strong, hefty piece to stand up to it over the long term. And, my God, have you *seen* some of the balls-to-the-walls loads they're coming out with in .40 S&W lately? It's like they're trying to turn this caliber into a full-power 10mm Auto! This ammo would beat the living hell out of a full-sized, steel-framed 1911 in short order, and I think slipping it into a 9mm sized platform is *really* pushing it. Of course, much of the attraction of the .40 S&W is that you can stuff a cartridge with a numerical designation beginning with a "4" into a gun the size of a 9mm. If it turns out this is not a good idea (and the more I learn, the more convinced I become that it is NOT), then the .40 S&W loses a lot of its appeal. Most people figure, "If I have to carry a gun the size of a .45 anyway, it might as well *be* a .45."

In many cases, guns chambered for .40 S&W do not have the greatest long-term durability in the world. That's because you're loading a round that generates .45-level recoil into guns initially designed to handle the recoil of a 9mm. Most .40 S&W handguns are in essence rebarreled 9mms, and when you whack a slide the mass of which was intended to dampen 9mm recoil with backbite equivalent to a .45, slide velocity gets so high that the gun swiftly begins to batter itself.

Now, there are guns that, when they were redesigned from 9mm to .40, attempted to address this problem. The most common method of doing so is to increase the weight of the weapon's slide and install a heavier recoil spring in an attempt to slow down slide travel. You might have noticed on the .40 Hi-Power that in order to adapt the basic P35 design to the more heavily recoiling caliber the slide was both widened and heightened, in the process adding considerable weight to dampen slide velocity. As a matter of fact, a good description of the .40 Hi-Power would be a P35 frame with a Colt .45 slide stuck on it! And this makes sense: if a gun is going to be chambered for a cartridge producing a recoil impulse equivalent to a .45, then it should probably have a slide the size of a .45 as well. On the other hand, in SIG-Sauer's .40-chambered P229 the designers were able to keep the slide basically the same size as the 9mm P228, but still add recoil-damping weight to the part by going to a solid, machined-steel slide on the .40, as opposed to the hollow stamping with pinned breech block used in the 9mm.

Now, someone in the audience is going to pop up with the fact that certain mini-.45s (such as the Colt Officer's ACPs) have slides both shorter and lighter than most .40s. And this is true. It is also true that in 1911-land the Officer's ACPs are not nearly as reliable or durable as the larger Commander- and Government Model-sized autos.

The guns I've seen most frequently give up the ghost under the pounding of .40 S&W recoil have been the Glock Models 23 and 27. Of course, this probably has a lot to do with the fact that many of the truly serious shooters in my area, the sort of people who pour a lot of rounds through their carry guns, are arming themselves with .40 Glocks. I consider this a regional phenomenon: many well-trained shooters tend to wind up carrying the same guns as their instructors, and in Washington state, where I reside, the two most successful firearms trainers are Greg Hamilton of InSights Training Center and Marty Hayes of the Firearms Academy of Seattle. For years, Greg carried a Glock 23, and Marty's carry gun is a Glock 22 with the butt cut down to the dimensions of a Glock 23.

Also, there has been no attempt, vis-à-vis going to a heavier recoil spring, to lessen battering in these guns. Glock uses the same weight-recoil spring in both its .40s and 9mms.

So, due to the area in which I live, I've had the opportunity to talk to many people who've put a considerable number of rounds through their .40 Glocks, to examine their guns after they've fired umpteen rounds, and to actually watch how these pieces performed at various handgun training classes I've attended. Frankly, after talking to those shooters who've carried and shot Glock 23s extensively, as well as interviewing the people at shooting ranges/gun shops who get to see exactly how these weapons hold up, I have to admit I'm a bit leery of the .40 Glocks (with the exception of the full-sized Glocks 22 and 24). These guns do not seem to hold up well under hard use. One Glock 23 in my area was battered into unserviceability after approximately 6,000 rounds!

What seems to happen on the guns I've seen that are shot heavily is that, where the front of the barrel hood mates with the front of the ejection port, the two surfaces start to peen each other; a lip of metal actually begins to rise up on both surfaces, which interferes with the gun going fully into battery. A very experienced shooter/instructor of my acquaintance explained his experience with his Glock 23 carry gun thus: "I was out at another instructor's training class, helping run the range, and I was doing a little shooting myself. I noticed that about one out of every 10 shots would hit 5 or 6 inches above the rest of my group. Well, I figured it wasn't *me* doing that, so I started watching the gun, and what I saw was that about once every 10 shots the barrel wouldn't go all the way into battery, so that round shot high." (Glocks, more so than most auto pistols, will fire out of battery.) "After that it started getting worse, to the point where the barrel was so far out of battery that you started getting off-center firing pin hits, and the gun started to misfire. I carried this gun for about three years, but I never really shot it that much. I'd say I had about 6,000 rounds through it when all this happened; certainly not more than 10,000." This shooter, by the way, has now switched to a 9mm-chambered Glock 19 for his carry gun with total satisfaction.

Glock's mini-.40, the Model 27, seems to hold up even more poorly than the G23. When this gun had been out for only a few months, one of our local gun shops had already had two of the things come back because they simply beat themselves to death. Now, the 9mm-chambered mini, the Glock 26, seems to be working great and holding up well. Similarly, the Glock 19, a gun nearly identical to the G23 save for its 9mm chambering, holds up just fine, far better than the G23. You don't see the problems of serious gun battering in a G19 that you do with the G23. The only .40 Glock I've seen that seems to have what it takes from the standpoint of long-term durability is the full-sized Model 22, which has enough mass in its full-length slide to slow down slide velocity to the point where the gun doesn't batter itself during the recoil cycle. I would assume the same to be true for Glock's competition-oriented Model 24 longslide; with the cutout nature of the G24's slide, it weighs exactly the same as the G22's.

Lest it seem like I'm picking on the Glocks, let me say that the G23/27's lack of long-term durability is not, I feel, something you can really blame on the Glock design per se. It is, rather, a basic flaw in the idea of shoving a hot, big bore cartridge into a gun the size of a reasonably smallish 9mm. And in fairness to the Glocks 23 and 27, we must acknowledge that these are not the only semi-small autos getting pounded by .40 S&W recoil. I'm also noticing some batter-ing in the SIG P229 (even with the heavier slide), especially on the recoil-spring guide rod, that's not occurring on the identically sized but 9mm-chambered P228. On any P229 that has been shot at all extensively, the flange on the end of the recoil-spring guide rod will swiftly bend itself backward at a 45-degree angle, and that simply doesn't happen on a SIG 9mm.

Another problem with the .40 S&W: this is a very high pressure cartridge with a very fast pressure spike. Because the .40 S&W is a big-bore cartridge, I think a lot of people have the attitude that it must be a pretty mild number with low chamber pressures, like the .45 ACP. Nothing could be further from the truth. SAAMI pressure limits for the .40 S&W are identical to those for the .357 Magnum. That is, 35,000 pounds per square inch (psi) for both calibers. Compare this to 17,000 psi for the non-+P .45 ACP. There has been no +P standard set by SAAMI for the .40 S&W, and that's primarily because the "stan-dard pressure" loads are riding so close to the edge to start with. Usually, all this means is that wear and tear on the gun is a lot more severe with .40s than many people would assume; however, in some cases these high operating pressures can cause more serious problems.

You may have heard the persistent rumors that .40-chambered Glocks will occasionally, for no apparent reason, blow up—and we're not talking with handloads either, but with factory ammo. When I first heard these tales myself I figured they were BS, or else the folks who had blown cases in their guns were using handloads and simply didn't want to admit it. Although that may well have been the case in a few instances, I kept hearing these stories from too many reliable sources not to realize that it was, indeed, actually happening on occasion. As I've come to learn more about Glocks in general, and the .40 S&W cartridge in particular, it's become obvious to me what's occurring here. There are a couple of factors at work:

(1) The barrels that come in Glocks are very, very good. They feature polygonal rifling (rather than standard lands and grooves), which confers a better gas seal behind the projectile, as well as less friction as a bullet travels down the bore. All else being equal, Glocks "shoot harder" than other guns, i.e., they fire the same loads to slightly higher velocities than when they're fired from identical-length but conventionally rifled barrels. Unfortunately, these barrels were designed to handle jacketed ammunition only; one of the few things they do not do well is fire lead ammo. Even hard-cast bullets, let alone softer projectiles, will swiftly coat a Glock's bore with a thick deposit of lead. This, of course, raises pressures tremendously because it increases resistance as a bullet tries to travel down the gunked up bore.

(2) As previously mentioned, the .40 S&W is a high-pressure cartridge, with a very fast pressure spike and top-end pressures equivalent to a .357 Magnum.

Add the foregoing two facts together, and it's easy to figure out what's happening in the .40 Glocks. When you fire lead ammo through the Glock's polygonally rifled barrel, pressures swiftly rise into the danger zone with the high-intensity .40 S&W chambering, so much so that sooner or later you wind up blowing a cartridge casing in the unsupported area over the feed ramp. Now, I'm not saying you should never fire lead ammo through your Glock .40 (although that *would* be my own inclination). What I *am* telling you is that if you fire your .40-chambered Glock extensively with lead ammo and then load up with hot factory stuff without first thoroughly cleaning the bore, you're asking for serious trouble.

I think the matter of blowing cases in a Glock would have achieved far less attention than it has (after all, people do it all the time in Colt .45s with incompetent handloads) but for the fact that it's just so *impressive* when a cartridge casing lets go inside the polymer framed Glock mechanism. I've had the opportunity to actually be there on the shooting line when a shooter blew a casing in his Glock (although this was a .45, not a .40), and it was most instructive. When a casing blows in a steel-framed 1911, amazingly, aside from a ruined magazine, usually nothing else is damaged, so you just stick another magazine in the gun to replace the ruined mag, pound the Pachmayrs back flat, and drive on. When the same thing happens in a Glock, it totally lunches the piece, splits the plastic frame longitudinally from the front of the dust cover to the bottom of the frontstrap, and blows the trigger out of the gun!

We might pause to ask ourselves why, of all the Glocks, the .40s seem to be prone to this sort of detonation. Well, I believe it's a combination of the high-intensity nature of the .40 S&W and this gun's suitability for IPSC competition, where shooters fire an incredible amount of lead ammo. The 9mms, although they operate at chamber pressures similar to the .40s, are commonly considered not suitable for IPSC because the chambering doesn't "make Major." Also, lead 9mm ammo is not common; the same could be said for the 10mm-chambered Glock 20. The .45 ACP-chambered G21 does offer a Major caliber, and lead ammo in .45 is common; however, this gun's huge grip limits its appeal to many shooters, and the .45 ACP is a low pressure cartridge to start with. This leaves the .40s as the only Glocks that offer decent-sized grips and a Major caliber that's loaded to very high pressures, for which lead ammunition is readily available (even without handloading: both Federal and Winchester produce lead ammo in .40 S&W).

I have examined a Glock 23 belonging to one of our local IPSC shooters in which the frame had literally shattered on both sides just in front of the locking block. This gun did not look safe to fire, and in fact I was able to take a look at the weapon just before it was shipped back to Glock for repair. I was amazed: I'd never seen that sort of damage before to a Glock's tough polymer frame. But then I asked what sort of ammo had been fired through this gun, and how much. The answer: "About 15,000 rounds, and it was just lead ammo, fairly lightly loaded." Ah-ha! Knowing what I know about how extensive firing of lead ammo can raise pressures in Glocks, and considering the infrequent cleaning most IPSC shooters give their guns, and that the .40 ammo fired was probably loaded to make Major, the idea of just how high pressures were running inside that gun with its "lightly loaded" ammo is enough to break me out in a chill sweat!

I've seen a lot of feed-reliability problems in guns chambered for .40 S&W. Part of this is caused by the fact that, as I discussed before, most guns in the caliber are, when you get right down to it, simply rebarreled 9mms. I believe it was former World IPSC champion Ray Chapman who pointed out that auto pistols tend to work best when chambered in the calibers for which they were originally designed. The length of an auto's slide stroke, the timing of its feed cycle, its spring compression ratios—all are designed around the recoil impulse and actual physical dimensions of a particular cartridge. When a gun is rechambered for a cartridge that is significantly longer or shorter, wider or narrower, or that produces significantly more or less recoil than what the gun was initially designed to work with, it is unlikely it will perform as well.

Also, the shape of most .40 S&W projectiles mitigates against their feeding reliably. I feel it is especially important, from a standpoint of feed reliability, to avoid loading your gun with ammo featuring a straight-sided, jacketed truncated-cone (JTC) bullet profile. When loaded with such ammunition, many auto pistols become quite prone to what pistolsmiths call "high angle jams." Basically, what happens during the feeding cycle on most auto pistols (ideally) is that the next round in the magazine slides out of the magazine feed lips, bounces up off the feed ramp, and then bounces again, down off the top of the chamber. By this time the round is far enough into the chamber that the action can snap shut around it. With JTC ammo what often happens is that, when the round bounces off the feed ramp and hits the top of the chamber, the straight chamber wall meets the straight side of the projectile and, instead of bouncing off, the round simply *stops*. What you wind up with is the cartridge out of the magazine but stuck halfway in the chamber, held there at a 45-degree angle. Glocks and 1911s seem especially prone to this sort of malfunction. As a matter of fact, the Environmental Protection Agency switched from the Glock 23 to the Glock 19 as its issue sidearm because of problems with failures to go into battery/high angle jams with the JTC-profile Federal Hydra-Shoks.

The bad news here is that ammo makers seem infatuated with the JTC bullet profile in .40 S&W caliber. There are only a few .40 S&W loads that feature a feed-reliable, rounded, hardball-like ogive. These would include the Winchester 155-grain Silvertips, Winchester 180-grain Black Talons (now sadly unavailable for civilian sales), and Winchester 180-grain JHPs (marketed as "Subsonic Deep Penetrators"). Winchester seems to be paying more attention to feed reliability in .40 S&W caliber than all the other ammo companies put together. With the exception of these hollowpoints produced by Winchester (and I could stand to be corrected on this), the only .40 S&W ammo I can think of that does not feature a JTC profile bullet is the Hansen 180-grain FMJ solid; this load's ogive is nice and rounded, albeit with a flat point.

Why does so much of the ammunition being currently produced in .40 S&W, as well as other auto pistol calibers, feature JTC profile bullets? It's because these days there is a heavy emphasis on designing handgun ammunition that will expand nicely in ballistic gelatin and, all else being equal, a bullet with a straight-sided JTC shape to it will expand more readily than a bullet with a more generously rounded ogive because, with the same size hollow cavity, the bullet walls are thinner. Now, this is all well and good (wonderful, as a matter of fact); however, when you start making ammo design decisions that negatively affect feed reliability just to impress a gelatin block, I would have to say that emphasis is being placed in the wrong area. I don't care how awesome a bullet is in gelatin (or even inside a human body, for that matter)—all that does you no good if your gun won't fire because it just choked on your wonderbullet! There is a reason, quite apart from the Hague Accords, that military handgun ammunition is full-metal-jacketed hardball, and that reason is feed reliability. I'm not saying you should load your defensive handgun with hardball. I *will* say that the more your ammunition departs from a rounded, hardball-like ogive, the more you're asking for trouble from a standpoint of feed reliability.

When I was interviewing Joseph Rousseau, the Browning engineer who, working with a team of engineers in Belgium, designed the .40 Hi-Power, he made a very insightful comment: that whenever a gun malfunctions people never blame the ammunition, they blame the gun. Well, the fact is that some ammo is so poorly designed, vis-à-vis its feed-reliability profile, that you really can't blame a gun for not wanting to swallow it! Unfortunately, in .40 S&W that statement covers just about everything in the caliber.

SUMMARY

So, is the .40 S&W really, in the world of the defensive handgun, the greatest thing since the invention of smokeless powder? Is it what some gunwriters have called it, "the combat handgun cartridge of the future"? God knows it looks like a great idea on the surface. But when we examine the concept more deeply, we begin to see problems. I hate being the one to point out that the emperor has no clothes (but, then again, *someone's* gotta do it!), and I am loath to seem like a reactionary, but frankly I think I'm gonna have to go the traditionalistic route here: if I want a gun that holds a lot of rounds I'll choose a 9mm, and if I want a big bore I'll take a .45!

CHAPTER EIGHT

DR. JEKYLL AND MR. HYDE VS. THE GOOD FAIRY

I knew myself, at the first breath of this new life, to be more wicked, tenfold more wicked, sold a slave to my original evil; and the thought, in that moment, braced and delighted me like wine.

—Robert Louis Stevenson
Dr. Jekyll and Mr. Hyde

"There's nothing left to believe in. Nothing!"
"Nothing, my dear? Oh, now you don't mean that."
"Oh, but I do!"
"Nonsense, child. If you'd lost all *your faith I couldn't be here. And here I am!"*
—Cinderella and the Fairy Godmother
Walt Disney's *Cinderella*

Two great myths (or maybe "logical errors" would be a better term) prevail when most people consider handguns. These are what I call the Dr. Jekyll and Mr. Hyde Theory and the Fairy Godmother Syndrome. The Dr. Jekyll and Mr. Hyde Theory is epitomized by the statement, "I don't want to have a gun around because I'm afraid I might kill someone I love in the middle of an argument." It's as if the person making that statement believes the gun is an evil talisman emitting invisible, personality-altering radiation, capable of twisting a well-adjusted, peaceful human being into a slavering killer by its very presence.

The Fairy Godmother Syndrome is evinced by those folks who

tell themselves, "I'm safe because I have a gun," as though the firearm is a beneficent entity, a good fairy actively capable of protecting them from harm, or perhaps a charmed sword that will automatically leap from its scabbard to do battle on their behalf.

In both cases, people have anthropomorphized the gun, ascribing to it human motivations and attributes it could not possibly possess. A handgun is not an evil talisman, nor is it a good fairy. A handgun is simply a tool: nothing more, nothing less. A handgun does (in alphabetical order) nada, nothing, zero, zilch, and zip by itself. It simply lies there, totally powerless, a dead, inert chunk of wood and metal, aluminum or plastic. It could lie there until everyone now living dies and turns to dust—until we're all as dead as if we'd lived in ancient Egypt—unless it's picked up and used by a human being. A gun will not do evil without a guiding will behind it. Similarly, it will not protect your life unless wielded with skill and determination by your own hands.

With the possible exception of the automobile, no material objects are such icons of power in the American consciousness as firearms. And of all firearms, the handgun elicits the most powerful, visceral response from people. It's the most personal of weapons. And that's too bad, really. When any object assumes such monumental import, becomes that wonderful, fearful, and awe inspiring in a person's eyes, his ability to calmly and dispassionately consider the pros and cons and the virtues and vices of said object tends to go out the window as he reacts on gut instinct. Many folks love their guns with a passion pure and true, while others regard a .38 revolver with all the horror of a Jehovah's Witness attending a pagan mass.

Just because guns won't act by themselves doesn't mean they're not powerful tools. You know, when I was a kid I read a book about a couple of boys who got their hands on a bottle filled with a magic substance called Ever So Much More Powder. Whenever anything was sprinkled with this wonderful stuff, whatever that object's defining characteristic might be was rendered, well, Ever So Much More. For instance, a lemon would become Ever So Much More sour, a long-haired dog would become Ever So Much More shaggy, and so on. Guns are like the Ever So Much More Powder in that whatever is inside a person, having a gun can give them Ever So Much More capability to project that internal reality outward. Depending on the person involved, the results can be horrific and destructive, but they can just as easily be heroic and life preserving. If your nature is to hurt and victimize others, a gun can indeed enhance your ability to do so. But if your instinct is to nurture and protect innocent life, including your own or the lives of those you love, then a gun can give you Ever So Much More potential to do *that* as well.

Obviously, I'm biased in this regard: I think handguns can be wonderful tools for preserving the lives and well-being of the innocent. If I didn't believe that, I wouldn't have made testing, writing about, and mastering them such a large part of my life's work. Still, for me handguns are tools, not icons of power, and I'm under no illusion that my gun will protect me unless directed by own volition and skill.

Amusing (and not at all uncharming) are those people who personalize their guns to the point of giving them names. I have a friend who does this, primarily as a game for his own amusement. He chooses his sidearms in part for their historical and esthetic characteristics (their personalities, in other words). And they all have names, many of them based on movie titles and cinematic characters, since my friend is also a serious film buff. Betty Blue, Vulnavia, Little Caesar, to name but a few, have all passed through his hands and holsters over the years. For me, by contrast, everything else takes a back seat to reliability and functionality. My friend and I recently had a diverting conversation on the topic of our personal carry guns. His was a Colt stainless-steel Delta Elite 10mm. Fondling his Delta, he said, "Well, I just love the Colt O-frame. I think it's the quintessential large American auto pistol design. And it may be foolish, but I like having the power of the 10mm available. It's my bear, Cadillac, and crocodile cartridge."

So I whipped out my Glock 19, and said, "You know, I'm not one of those people who thinks there's one perfect handgun for everyone, but for my *own* use I'm finding it hard to imagine a gun that could suit me better than the Glock 19. It's lightweight (30 ounces fully loaded—that's less than most tactically equivalent handguns weigh unloaded); it's compact (we're talkin' a gun that's really not that

much larger than a Colt Detective Special when you take into account
the oversized rubber grips the factory's putting on Dick Specials these
days, but the G19 gives you the handling qualities and magazine
capacity of a full-sized service autoloader); it's got a short, light, consistent trigger pull, which is a nice feature; it's got high magazine
capacity; it's got no sharp edges to cut up your hands while firing it
or your clothing while carrying it concealed; and it's a very self-contained design with no major openings into the action, so you don't
really have to worry too much about crud working its way into the
mechanism. By my standards, it's just about the perfect handgun."

"And it has a plastic soul," said my friend, with fastidious disdain.

"Well, in my opinion, handguns don't *have* souls, plastic or otherwise. They're just tools. And whatever else you can say about
Glocks, when you get one that works 100 percent of the time, you've
got a supremely functional tool."

But to each his own. I do have to say, though, that while I can
understand the regard a craftsman has for a superior tool, one that
does its work well and never lets him down (and I do feel a bit of that
for my Glock), I've never felt the slightest desire to name it like a
newborn baby. I think "serial number BKR 766" or possibly "my
Glock 19" suffices for a name. Of course, Jim Cirillo, survivor of
numerous life-or-death gun battles during his days with the legendary New York City Police Stakeout Squad, tells me he's never
even gotten that fancy—"my gun" has always worked for him!

GUN TRIVIA

If a man insisted always on being serious, and never allowed
himself a bit of fun and relaxation, he would go quite mad or
become unstable without realizing it.

—Herodotus

I thought it might be fun to have the last chapter in this book be a list of gun trivia questions. It may be argued (with some logic) that gun trivia does not fall under the category of "handgun myths." And that is true. It is also true that fun doesn't have to be logical!

For years *Guns & Ammo* magazine has been running its own gun trivia column, but the questions contained therein have always struck me as being extremely technical and esoteric. In this section instead I'll try to focus on things that might actually be within the knowledge (and interest) of the average gun owner. I'm going to give you the questions by themselves and then the answers in a separate section. No peeking unless absolutely necessary!

GUN TRIVIA QUESTIONS

1. In Jerry Ahern's *Survivalist* series of adventure novels, what two handguns are always carried by the character of John Rourke, and how does he carry them?

2. What handgun was carried by Shaft?

3. What handgun was carried by Maxwell Smart?

4. What handgun was carried by Napoleon Solo in the original *Man from U.N.C.L.E.* television series?

5. What fictional San Francisco police inspector carries a Smith & Wesson Model 29 .44 Magnum?

6. In the movie *Tightrope*, what handgun does the Clint Eastwood character carry?

7. What two handguns did The Shadow carry?

8. Who loaded his pearl-handled Colt Single-Action Army .45s with silver bullets?

9. Since a Smith & Wesson Model 29 .44 Magnum was not available for Clint Eastwood to carry in the first Dirty Harry film, with what firearm, by model and caliber, did Hollywood propmasters actually outfit him?

10. In the television series *The Rockford Files*, what handgun does Jim Rockford keep in his trailer by the sea, and why does he keep it buried up to its hammer in a jar of coffee?

11. In the first Dirty Harry film, how many rounds had Harry Callahan actually fired out of his .44 *before* he killed the Scorpio killer?

12. List three common names for the service autoloader adopted by the German army in 1908.

13. Who designed the Gatling gun?

14. By what name is the aircraft-mounted machine gun called that is basically a Gatling gun hooked to an electric motor?

15. What weapon was used by the Son of Sam killer?

16. Who invented the derringer?

17. What handgun was used to assassinate Archduke Franz Ferdinand, precipitating World War I?

18. What was the make and caliber of the gun with which Ian Fleming *originally* armed James Bond?

19. For what caliber was James Bond's Walther PPK chambered?
20. By what name is the 9mm Kurz cartridge commonly referred to in the United States?
21. How many rounds does a Smith & Wesson Chief's Special hold?
22. How many rounds does a Colt Detective Special hold?
23. What is the standard magazine capacity of the Colt Government Model .45 auto?
24. By what name is the gun referred to in Europe as the P.08 or Parabellum commonly called in the United States? (Clue: The name, as it refers to this gun, is a trademark of the U.S. importer, A.F. Stoeger, Inc.)
25. What gun did Mike Hammer carry?
26. In *I, the Jury*, after Mike Hammer's normal carry gun is taken away by the police as evidence in a murder, with what weapon does Hammer rearm himself?
27. What did Mike Hammer call shooting and killing someone?
28. What handgun did Colt advertise as holding the "all-important sixth shot"?
29. In what year was the Colt Detective Special introduced?
30. List at least two names by which the Browning Hi-Power is called in Europe.
31. After the West German police service pistol trials of the mid-1970s, when all the "acceptable" police handguns were given "P" (*Pistole*) designations, what name was given to the Heckler & Koch PSP?
32. After the West German police service pistol trials, what name was given to the SIG-Sauer P225?
33. By what name is the Grande Puissance commonly referred to in the United States?
34. In what year was the Browning Hi-Power first marketed in .40 S&W caliber?
35. What is the most common nickname for the 158-grain lead semi-wadcutter hollowpoint +P .38 Special handgun cartridge?
36. By what nickname is the 158-grain lead semi-wadcutter hol-

lowpoint +P .38 Special handgun cartridge commonly known in Chicago and why?

37. What handgun did John Hinkley use in his assassination attempt on Ronald Reagan?

38. With what handgun did Sirhan Sirhan kill Robert Kennedy?

39. With what handgun did Mark David Chapman kill John Lennon?

40. In what Beatles tune is found the lyrics "happiness is a warm gun"?

41. What Beatles album has as its title the name of a type of firearm?

42. What weapon was used in two assassination attempts on President Gerald Ford?

43. How many rounds did Mike Hammer carry in his Colt .45?

44. How did Mike Hammer carry his Colt .45 auto?

45. In the Ian Fleming novel *Doctor No*, what description was given of the stopping characteristics of James Bond's new Walther PPK?

46. What did Josh Randall call his cut-down .45-70?

47. What does the U.S. Army call the Colt .45 Government Model?

48. What does the U.S. Army call the Beretta Model 92?

49. What does the U.S. Army call the SIG-Sauer P228?

50. What does the U.S. Army call the Colt AR-15?

51. Who designed the Garand rifle?

52. In what year did firearms designer John Browning die?

53. What was firearms designer John Browning's middle name?

54. What does BAR stand for?

55. What was the primary difference in the custom Smith & Wesson Model 27 conversions offered by the Baumannize company as compared to a stock gun?

56. How many rounds does a Harrington & Richardson Model 999 revolver hold?

57. In the comics, what gun was used to kill Bruce Wayne's parents, causing him to become The Batman?

58. What is Superman faster than?

59. In the *Twin Peaks* television show, what did Leo Johnson tell Laura Palmer when he stuck a $1,000 poker chip in her mouth?
60. Who invented the Pepper Popper?
61. What is the caliber of Harry Callahan's revolver?
62. According to Harry Callahan, what is "the most powerful handgun in the world"? Give the maker and model designation.
63. In the movie *Alien Nation*, after his 9mm fails to stop a drug-crazed alien fast enough for his tastes, what firearm does James Caan start carrying instead?
64. With what firearm did Medal of Honor recipient Alvin York stop a German squad bayonet charge?
65. What is the handgun most associated with Britain's elite Special Air Services?
66. How many rounds does the Charter Arms Bulldog .44 Special hold?
67. In the original *Star Trek* television series, how many types of phasers appeared, and what were they?
68. What sort of handguns do Klingons carry?
69. According to science fiction writer/philosopher Robert Heinlein, what does an armed society make?
70. What famous star of a firearms-related television series played baseball for the Dodgers before becoming an actor?
71. What title of an episode of the original *Star Trek* television series features the name of a firearm?
72. Of what organization did science fiction writer/philosopher Robert Heinlein write, "I am very proud to be a member of . . ."
73. In the original *Star Trek* television series, what was the name of the only episode in which the phaser rifle appeared?
74. What do the initials JPSA stand for?
75. Name the person from whom came the statement, "Firearms stand next in importance to the Constitution itself. They are the American people's liberty teeth and keystone under independence."
76. What was John Browning's last pistol design, uncompleted at the time of his death?

77. In what country is Fabrique Nationale located?
78. In what year did SIG produce its first firearms?
79. What is the oldest company in the world still producing the type of product it originally began manufacturing?
80. In the television series *Baretta*, what two handguns does the main character regularly carry?
81. What do the initials ACP stand for?
82. In what country is SIG's corporate headquarters located?
83. In what country is the Beretta parent factory located?
84. What was the only country in World War II to arm itself with a handgun chambered for .380 ACP as primary service standard?
85. What happens when you open the action on a Webley revolver?
86. In which direction does the thumb safety on a Colt .45 auto move to make the gun ready to fire?
87. In which direction does the thumb safety on a traditional mechanism Smith & Wesson auto pistol move to make the gun ready to fire?
88. In which direction does the thumb safety on a Makarov move to make the gun ready to fire?
89. In which direction does the thumb safety on a Colt .45 auto move to make the gun safe?
90. In which direction does the thumb safety on a traditional mechanism Smith & Wesson auto move to drop a cocked hammer and make the gun safe?
91. In which direction does the thumb safety on a Makarov move to drop the cocked hammer and make the gun safe?
92. In which direction do you push the cylinder-release latch on a modern Smith & Wesson revolver to open up the action?
93. In which direction do you push the cylinder-release latch on a modern Colt revolver to open up the action?
94. In which direction do you push the cylinder-release latch on a Ruger DA revolver to open the action?
95. In what year was the Browning Hi-Power first marketed?
96. After John Browning's death, who completed and perfected the design for the Browning Hi-Power?

97. What does Colt call the swing-up portion of the recoil shield that is flipped up and out of the way to enable cartridges to be loaded into the Single-Action Army revolver?

98. What distinguishing feature do the Beretta Models 950BS, 21A, and 86 all have in common?

99. In the post World War II era, the U.S. Army conducted trials to find a new auto pistol to replace the M1911A1; the military eventually decided not to go to a new handgun at that time, but two weapons designed specifically for these tests were offered, quite successfully, on the commercial market. Name them both.

100. What is the only difference between a Colt Commander and a Colt Combat Commander?

101. By what other name is the Colt Commander commonly known?

102. What is the standard magazine capacity of the Detonics Combat Master, the Star PD, and the Colt Officers ACP compact .45 autos?

103. What handgun does Modesty Blaise carry in her early adventures?

104. In the Peter O'Donnell novel *Dragon's Claw*, what handgun does Modesty Blaise switch over to for her carry gun?

105. Who designed the Star PD?

106. Who designed the Detonics Combat Master?

107. In 1927, the "Colt .22 Automatic Target Pistol" began to be marketed under what name?

108. What handguns did the Lone Ranger carry?

109. What is the nickname for the Colt Single-Action Army revolver?

110. What is the most common chambering of the L.A.R. Grizzly auto pistol?

111. In what caliber was the Desert Eagle originally offered?

112. What company makes the Desert Eagle?

113. Where does PMC ammo come from?

114. Where does Fiocchi ammo come from?

115. What was the original name for the IMI Baby Eagle?

116. What will happen if you force a loaded Glock into the original-design plastic carrying case?

117. What will happen if you squeeze the trigger on a 1911-pattern auto, hold it to the rear, and flip off the thumb safety?
118. What will happen if you squeeze the trigger on an HK P7, hold it to the rear, and depress the squeeze cocker?
119. What does HK stand for?
120. What does HK call the safety system on the P7?
121. What does Glock call its trigger system?
122. What famous ammunition type was designed by the late Col. Jack Cannon?
123. What was the name of Lee Jurras' ammo company?
124. What ammo company is owned by Peter Pi?
125. What ammo company is owned by Jeff Hoffman?
126. What is the only ammo company in the world producing factory new .455 Webley cartridges?
127. In IPSC, what power factor "makes Major"?
128. In IPSC, what power factor "makes Minor"?
129. For what caliber is the Colt Delta Elite chambered?
130. What caliber was first chambered in the Bren Ten?
131. What caliber was first chambered in the Parabellum pistol?
132. What caliber was first chambered in the M1911 Colt Government Model?
133. What does FMJ stand for?
134. What does TMJ stand for?
135. What is the difference between an FMJ and a TMJ bullet?
136. Who made the original aluminum alloy frames for Colt Commanders?
137. What does S&W stand for?
138. What does AMT stand for?
139. What is the nickname for full-metal-jacketed, rounded-nosed military ammunition?
140. Why is military ammo, even pointy rifle cartridges, always called "ball"?
141. What Stanley Kubrick film takes its title from a type of military ammunition?
142. List four common names for the caliber chambered in the Smith & Wesson Model 3913.

143. By what commercial name is the 7.62x51mm NATO round sold in the United States?
144. What does SWC stand for?
145. What does LSWC stand for?
146. There are three possible meanings to the abbreviation "+P". Name them.
147. In the first *Lethal Weapon* movie, in order to show off his skill with a handgun, what does Martin Riggs do on the police firing range?
148. In the movie *Terminator*, what auto pistol does Arnold Schwarzenegger carry?
149. In the movie *Terminator*, what shotgun does Arnold Schwarzenegger carry?
150. In the movie *Terminator*, what submachine gun does Arnold Schwarzenegger carry?
151. In the movie *Terminator*, what firearm does Kyle Reese use against the Terminator, how did he get it, and how did he modify it after he acquired it?
152. In the movie *Terminator II*, what is the last weapon with which the T1000 Terminator is shot before being destroyed?
153. In *Terminator II*, what handgun does Sarah Connor carry for most of the film, before giving it to the T800 Terminator near the end of the movie?
154. In the first Rambo film, what weapon does Sylvester Stallone use to destroy a police station near the end of the film?
155. In the second Rambo film, what weapon does Sylvester Stallone drop into the mud when he is captured by Vietnamese soldiers?
156. In the second Rambo film, what handgun is the Vietnamese officer firing at Rambo when he gets hit with an exploding arrow?
157. In abbreviations for types of bullets, what does the letter "L" stand for?
158. Who wrote, "Shooting a gun that doesn't kick is like making love to a woman who just lies there."
159. Who said, "I forgot to duck, Mama"?
160. In the Stephen King novel *The Dark Tower III: The*

Wastelands, in 1977 Jake Chambers steals what nonexistent handgun from his father's desk drawer?

161. In the Stephen King short novel *The Mist*, what two handguns does Ollie Weeks say he owns?

162. In the Stephen King novel *The Tommyknockers*, with what handgun does Jim Gardener wind up fighting a group of genetically altered townspeople, only to be overwhelmed when the gun consistently misfires due to being loaded with decades-old ammunition?

163. In the first paragraph of the Dean Koontz novel *Watchers*, on his 36th birthday Travis Cornell gets ready to go hiking through a rural canyon in Southern California. He takes with him only three things. Name them.

164. When Colt introduced the Detective Special in 1926, it was simply a short-barreled version of what popular firearm?

165. In the novel *Logan's Run*, the most advanced hand weapon ever designed is called what?

166. In the novel *Logan's Run*, the sidearm of the Sandmen is styled to resemble what handgun?

167. In the novel *Logan's Run*, the handguns carried by the Sandmen have six possible functions. Name them.

168. According to the Beatles, happiness is what?

169. In the Stephen King "Bachman book" *Roadwork*, Bart Dawes buys two firearms in order to barricade himself inside his home to fight it out with the construction crew that is coming to tear down the house. What are they?

170. In the Stephen King short novel *The Body*, what handgun does Chris Chambers steal from his dad to take on the trip to find the body?

171. In the Stephen King short novel *The Mist*, how many rounds are left in David Drayton's .38 revolver at the end of the story?

172. In *The Dark Tower*, the first Stephen King Gunslinger novel, how many guns does Roland normally carry?

173. What injury occurs to Roland the Gunslinger at the beginning of the Stephen King novel *The Dark Tower II: The Drawing of the Three* that severely handicaps his gunfighting abilities?

174. John Steinbeck wrote, "The final weapon is . . ." what?
175. In the *Star Wars* movies, on what real-life handgun is Han Solo's laser pistol based?
176. In the Arnold Schwarzenegger film *Red Heat*, for what fictional handgun caliber is the main character's Russian handgun chambered?
177. In the Arnold Schwarzenegger film *Red Heat*, on what real-life auto pistol is the main character's handgun based?
178. In the television series *Starsky and Hutch*, what handgun did Starsky carry?
179. In the television series *Starsky and Hutch*, what handgun did Hutch carry?
180. For what ballistic reason did the Lone Ranger have his bullets made of silver?
181. How is K-O-C-H (as in Heckler & Koch) pronounced?

GUN TRIVIA ANSWERS

1. Two stainless-steel Detonics Combat Master .45s carried in an Alessi double shoulder rig
2. Smith & Wesson Model 60, stainless steel Chief's Special
3. Smith & Wesson Model 36, blued-steel Chief's Special
4. A silenced Walther P38K
5. Inspector Harry Callahan
6. A customized Smith & Wesson Model 66 .357 Magnum
7. Two Colt .45 Government Models
8. The Lone Ranger
9. A Smith & Wesson Model 57 .41 Magnum
10. A Smith & Wesson Model 36 Chief's Special .38; because "the coffee grounds stop the salt air from rusting it"
11. Five
12. The Luger, the P.08, and the Parabellum
13. Dr. Richard Gatling
14. The Vulcan
15. The Charter Arms .44 Special Bulldog
16. Henry Deringer, Jr.

17. Browning Model 1900, .32 ACP caliber
18. A Beretta .25
19. .32 ACP
20. The .380 ACP
21. Five
22. Six
23. Seven
24. The Luger
25. A Colt Government Model .45 auto
26. A Luger
27. Punching their ticket one way down the long highway
28. The Colt Detective Special
29. 1926
30. The Grande Puissance, the M1935, the P-35, the GP-35
31. The P7
32. The P6
33. The Browning Hi-Power
34. 1994
35. The FBI Load
36. The Metro Load, because the Chicago Metropolitan Police was the first major agency in the state to adopt it
37. The RG-14 .22 Long Rifle
38. The Iver Johnson Cadet M55 .22 Long Rifle
39. The Charter Arms Undercover .38 Special
40. "Happiness Is a Warm Gun"
41. *Revolver*
42. The Colt .45 Government Model auto
43. Six
44. In a shoulder holster
45. "It's a real stopping gun." NOTE: This is a bit of a trick question if you didn't read it closely. In the *movie* based on the novel, as the Armorer hands Bond his new gun he says, "Walther PPK, seven-point-six-five-mil, with a delivery like a brick through a plate-glass window." However, I asked about the *novel*, not the movie.
46. His "mare's leg"

47. The M1911 or M1911A1
48. The M9
49. The M11
50. The M16, M16A1, or M16A2
51. John C. Garand
52. 1926
53. Moses
54. Browning Automatic Rifle
55. The guns were fitted with cylinders that held seven rounds.
56. Nine
57. The Colt .45 Government Model
58. A speeding bullet
59. "Bite the bullet, baby."
60. John Pepper
61. .44 Magnum
62. The Smith & Wesson Model 29
63. The Freedom Arms .454 Casull revolver
64. The Colt .45 Government Model auto
65. The Browning Hi-Power
66. Five
67. Three: Phaser Number One, Phaser Number Two, and a phaser rifle
68. Klingon disruptors
69. "An armed society is a polite society."
70. Chuck Connors
71. "Spectre of the Gun"
72. The American Rifle Association
73. "Where No Man Has Gone Before"
74. Jews for the Preservation of the Second Amendment
75. George Washington
76. The Browning Hi-Power
77. Belgium
78. 1860
79. Beretta
80. Two blued-steel Smith & Wesson Model 36 Chief's Specials
81. Automatic Colt Pistol

82. Switzerland
83. Italy
84. Italy
85. It automatically ejects all the cartridges (or cartridge casings) with which it is loaded.
86. Down
87. Up
88. Down
89. Up
90. Down
91. Up
92. Forward
93. Rearward
94. Inward
95. 1935
96. Dieudonne Saive
97. The loading gate
98. Tip-up barrels that allow a cartridge to be placed directly into the chamber by hand
99. The Smith & Wesson Model 39 9mm and the Colt Commander .45
100. The Commander has an aluminum alloy frame, the Combat Commander has a steel frame.
101. The Colt Lightweight Commander
102. Six rounds
103. A Colt .32 revolver
104. The Star PD .45 auto
105. Pete Dickey
106. Sid Woodcock
107. The Woodsman
108. Twin pearl-handled Colt Single-Action Army .45s
109. The Peacemaker
110. .45 Winchester Magnum
111. .357 Magnum
112. Israeli Military Industries
113. South Korea

114. Italy

115. The Jericho

116. The gun will fire.

117. The gun will fire.

118. The gun will fire.

119. Heckler and Koch

120. The "continuous motion system"

121. The "Safe Action"

122. The Glaser Safety Slug

123. Super Vel

124. Cor-Bon

125. Black Hills

126. Fiocchi

127. 175

128. 125

129. 10mm Auto

130. 10mm Auto

131. 7.65mm Luger, aka .30 Luger

132. .45 ACP

133. Full metal jacket

134. Total metal jacket

135. On a full-metal-jacket bullet the copper jacket does not cover the bottom of the bullet, but instead leaves the lead exposed; on a total-metal-jacket bullet the entire bullet is jacketed, even the bottom.

136. The Aluminum Company of America (ALCOA)

137. Smith & Wesson

138. Arcadia Machine and Tool

139. Hardball

140. It's a holdover from black powder days when military projectiles were actually ball-shaped.
141. *Full Metal Jacket*
142. 9mm Parabellum, 9mm Luger, 9x19mm, and 9mm NATO
143. The .308 Winchester
144. Semi-wadcutter
145. Lead semi-wadcutter
146. Plus pressure, plus power, and plus powder
147. He puts his target all the way at the end of the range and then shoots a "smiley face" into the head of the target.
148. A longslide AMT Hardballer .45 auto fitted with a laser
149. The Franchi SPAS-12
150. An Uzi
151. A Remington 870 12-gauge pump shotgun, sawn off at barrel and butt, stolen from a police car
152. An M79 grenade launcher
153. A custom Colt .45 Government Model
154. An M60 light machine gun
155. An AK-47
156. A Browning Hi-Power
157. Lead
158. Massad Ayoob
159. Ronald Reagan, explaining to his wife Nancy how he happened to get shot
160. A ".44 Ruger automatic"
161. "I have a Colt .45 and a Llama .25."
162. A Colt .45 Government Model
163. "He took only a package of Oreo cookies, a large canteen full of orange-flavored Kool-Aid, and a fully loaded Smith & Wesson .38 Chief's Special."
164. The Police Positive Special
165. The Gun
166. The Colt Single-Action Army
167. Tangler, ripper, needler, nitro, vapor, and homer
168. A warm gun

169. A "four-sixty Weatherbee" rifle and a ".44 Magnum, the gun Dirty Harry had carried in that movie." NOTE: "Weatherbee" is King's spelling, gang, not mine!

170. A .45 auto, I would assume a Government Model (that's certainly what they used in the movie *Stand By Me*, based on *The Body*). The passage from the story reads:

> Chris had unslung his pack and opened it and reached inside. Now he was holding out a huge pistol with dark wood grips.
>
> "You wanna be the Lone Ranger or the Cisco Kid?" Chris asked, grinning.
>
> "Walking, talking Jesus! Where'd you get that?"
>
> "Hawked it out of my dad's bureau. It's a forty-five."
>
> "Yeah, I can see that," I said, although it could have been a .38 or a .357 for all I knew—in spite of all the John D. MacDonalds and Ed McBains I'd read, the only pistol I'd ever seen up close was the one Constable Bannerman carried . . . and although all the kids asked him to take it out of its holster, Bannerman never would.

171. Three
172. Two
173. He loses the first two fingers of his right hand.
174. ". . . the mind."
175. The Broomhandle Mauser
176. Podbyrin 9.2mm
177. The Desert Eagle .357 Magnum
178. A Smith & Wesson Model 59 9mm auto
179. A 6-inch barreled Colt Python .357 Magnum revolver
180. The purity of the metal made his bullets more accurate.
181. Coke

CITY SLICKERS AND GUN NUTS

"The time has come," the Walrus said,
"To talk of many things:
Of shoes—and ships—and sealing wax—
Of cabbages—and kings—
And why the sea is boiling hot—
And whether pigs have wings."

—Lewis Carroll
Through the Looking-Glass

I have a friend who just *loves* arguing about handgun stopping power. Which handgun load is best? Which caliber? The perennial .45 versus 9mm debate is a personal favorite. Damn, *every time* I see this guy he wants to talk about whether the .45's better than the 9mm! Myself, I figured out years ago that all either of 'em really does is make holes, and after that I lost interest. I couldn't for the life of me see what he accomplished with all that wasted breath. After all, it's not like we ever solve anything; he'll just be arguing about it all again the next time we get together . . . over and over. (As it was in the beginning, is now, and ever shall be, world without end. Amen.) *Why*, I asked myself. *What a waste of time!*

It took a note from a frequent and valued correspondent, L. Bruce Pond of Woodland, Georgia, to finally clue me in to what was happening here. In Bruce's letter, after relating a little family gossip about how

his son-in-law Jeff, daughter Kathy, and new baby granddaughter Mary
had been living with him and his wife for awhile, he commented:

> Having Jeff here has given me an insight into gun magazines and our
> reactions to them. On the surface, Jeff seems to be a bona fide gun nut, but
> he isn't. He shoots as much as possible with both his Ruger 9mm DAO and
> Kel-Tec, but sees them as tools. The practice is to make him a better shot
> and give himself an edge in defense. Anyway, I was having a duck over
> Taylor's treatment of the S&W Model 19 in the September *Handguns*. I
> was most unhappy over his statement that the 19 was "totally uncontrol-
> lable and instantly painful to shoot with full-power loads," at the same
> time, of course, pushing the 1911 .45 with ball ammo as God's gift to com-
> bat shooters. Jeff laughed and said, "You know, Dad, he's about as fair to
> your beloved 19 as you'd be to his .45 if you were writing the article."
>
> He was too right for me to argue with him, so I laughed and agreed
> with him. He went on, "I'm not into gun mags like you, but it seems to
> me that they're all alike. All agree that handguns are far from ideal for
> defense, and even with center hits are underpowered for the job. Even you
> admit that there isn't a nickel's worth of difference between the so-called
> serious handgun loads and guns. Still you all separate into various groups
> and seem to enjoy defending your opinions to the last word. At the same
> time, if one of the people you're arguing with has a problem you all jump
> in to help. There have been times when the arguments seemed hot enough
> to start a gunfight, then in two minutes you're all loaning ear protection to
> a .45 shooter and shooting side by side like the old friends you are.
>
> "I think the whole argument is a sham that you all play like a game.
> Otherwise how could all of these magazines be sold when they all say the
> same thing every month? You can't tell me that Taylor didn't know he was
> writing fighting words there. Nor can you say that you didn't know what
> he would write when comparing the .45 to the .357. So why did you read
> it? I'll bet that if Taylor got into trouble you'd go five miles out of your
> way to help him. The both of you would argue all the way back, for you're
> all family and you argue for the fun of it."
>
> You know, Duane, we've talked of this in the past, and Jeff has us
> pegged, doesn't he? Anyway, you, Chuck Taylor, Jan Libourel, et al, keep
> writing and we'll keep buying. Why? Because it's a lot of fun.

And suddenly my friend's constant rehashing of the .45 versus 9mm debate, which never resolves anything but seems to give him such pleasure, made a lot more sense to me. It's a way of communicating . . . in an "approved," appropriately macho fashion, of course. ("What, I just want someone to talk to, the comfort of human companionship? Get away from me with that namby-pamby psycobabble bullshit: I'm talkin' about *guns* here, man!" We pause to knock back a healthy belt of testosterone.) Remember the scene in the Billy Crystal movie *City Slickers*, when Helen Slater asks the three old friends who are the film's main characters why so many men know so much about baseball, not just the teams or who won last year's World Series, but the most obscure statistics? And one of the guys (whom we've learned previously in the film had a very nasty relationship with his father) looks thoughtful and says something to the effect of, "You know, no matter how bad things got between me and my dad . . . we could always talk about baseball." It is in that spirit of communication this book has been written and offered to you—in an appropriately macho fashion, of course.

Most of the arguments over which we gun nuts so love haranguing each other (revolver versus auto pistol, single-action autos versus double-action autos, the 9mm versus .45 versus .357 Magnum, etc.) have been worn smooth from much handling, so much so any fire that might originally have burned within them is long gone, and now they have the force and comfort of rituals. (Thank God the .40 S&W Versus Everything debate's come along to keep things fresh!)

That's not to say there aren't some people out there who *really* believe all this stuff is monstrously important and actually get extremely angry and upset over it. Oh well, to each his own; there's not too much I can do about that, I guess. I don't offer intensive psychotherapy; I'm just a gunwriter.

Well, we're almost done, faithful reader. Thank you for sticking with me this far. As the curtain begins to fall, the stage lights dim, and it comes time to say good-bye, I might leave you with this one thought: you know, on occasion when someone asks my take on a particular topic and I give them an answer that differs from his own beliefs, he'll glare at me and accuse, "Well, that's just *your* opinion."

He's perfectly right, of course. What I write is my opinions, based on my experiences. I think I can do a pretty good job of logically justifying my beliefs based on the facts, but I'm realistic enough to understand that just because I believe something doesn't mean it came down from Mount Sinai carved into stone tablets. You may have opinions and beliefs, experiences and predilections that differ from my own. And that's fine. It would certainly be a boring world if everyone agreed about everything!

I hope you've had as much fun reading this book as I had writing it. Who knows, if you really enjoyed it, maybe we can do it again someday.

BIBLIOGRAPHY

Lee, David D. *Sergeant York: An American Hero*. Lexington, KY: University Press of Kentucky, 1985.

Lott, Jack. "Incident at Bridge 14." *Handguns*. Nov. 1990.

Marshall, Evan and Ed Sanow. *Handgun Stopping Power*. Boulder, CO: Paladin Press, 1992.

Marshall, Evan and Ed Sanow. *Street Stoppers*. Boulder, CO: Paladin Press, 1996.

McBride, Herbert W. *A Rifleman Went to War*. Marines, NC: Small-Arms Technical Publishing Company, 1935. (Reprinted by Lancer Militaria, Mount Ida, AR, 1987.)

Skeyhill, Tom. *Sergeant York, His Own Life Story and War Diary*. Garden City, NY: Doubleday, Doran & Company, 1928.

Thomas, Duane. "Handgun Myths Exploded." *Handguns*. Sept. 1996.

DEDICATION

I suppose on some level I've always known I wanted to be a writer. It just took me 25 years to realize it consciously. As a child in grade school I remember reading novels and analyzing how the writers achieved particular effects, the structure of the book, the tricks of the trade, never dreaming at the time that one day I'd be making my living at the craft of writing.

It's a strange thing I've noticed, but if you were to ask people, "What would you do for a living if you could do *anything?* Forget for a moment whether you think it's possible, whether you have the training, or the money, or the talent, or the intelligence; for the moment that doesn't matter. If you could do anything, what would it be?" most people could tell you. The sad part is it's almost never what they're actually doing. But it's almost never something impossible, either—it's something they *could* be doing if they really wanted to.

I spent 10 years on active duty in the United States Army. Of course, I'm not BSin' anyone here (no "Well, during my fifth Nam tour . . ." stories), I was an MOS 71L2P (for those of you not up on military-speak, that translates into Administrative Sergeant, read "clerk typist"). Oddly enough, just like you see in the TV commercials, my military training did come in really handy in my civilian job once I got out. I left the Army able to type 100-plus words a minute (after 10 years of doing it for hours on end almost every day it would've been amazing if I *couldn't*), which is definitely a handy skill to have as a free-lance writer!

My first three years in the Army I was an, ahem!, Airborne paratrooper stationed at Fort Bragg (that's where the "P" in my MOS came from; it stands for "paratrooper qualified"—Thomas' Helpful Home Facts Number 307) . . . of course, I was also a clerk in the Airborne! Now, even Airborne clerks gotta jump out of airplanes, and I did my fair share of forced marches and night combat equipment jumps, but I would mislead you if I did not admit I spent the vast majority of my time in the Airborne sitting on my butt in front of a word processor with my ankle chained to the desk. Even paratroopers need their letters typed, and not all Airborne soldiers are infantrymen: there are Airborne clerks, cooks, grease monkeys, commo rats, you name it—anything a unit needs to keep itself up and running. In case you've ever wondered what the hardest part is about being an Airborne clerk typist, I'll tell you: it's holding your typewriter at Port Arms as you exit the aircraft—centrifugal force wants to rip it right out of your hands!

But I digress. Understand that in this next bit of life history I'm not putting down the military. For some people it's a great deal, and there was a time in my life when it allowed me opportunities I wouldn't otherwise have had (like running away from home, for one). But after my first six years or so in the Mean Green Machine, it became blindingly obvious to me that this was not what I wanted to do for 20 or 30 years of my life. What I *did* want to do was take a crack at making my living as a free-lance writer . . . but I didn't have the guts to try because it would've hurt too much to fail.

Standard advice to beginning writers is, "Write what you know."

Well, I've loved guns, especially handguns, since I was a rugrat poring over my father's well-thrashed copy of the 1972 *Shooter's Bible*. There were only a few things in the world I really knew a lot about, enough to write on intelligently, and one of them was handguns. So people asked me, "Well, why don't you try writing about guns?" to which I replied, "Yeah, right . . . like I could make a living doing *that!*"

Well, one day there I was in my unit, sitting in front of my word processor as always (though honesty compels me to admit they did occasionally undo the leg chain to let me eat and sleep), thinking about how much I wanted to be a writer and how scared I was to try, and suddenly I had this *horrible* vision of myself as an old man of 83, looking back on my life and realizing I'd never had the guts to even *try* the one thing I really wanted to do the most. And I realized that not trying was just failing by omission. So before I could lose my nerve, I put my fingers on the keyboard, started typing, and in one session wrote my first gun article. It was a little three-pager, a piece of short fiction entitled "The First Annual Combat Handgun Expert's Free Dinner and Ceremonial Bash," my attempt at a humorous short-short story recounting what might happen if some of the more famous gunwriters happened to be all together in one room, soaking up some free suds and eats, when two shotgun-wielding thugs broke into the room and tried to execute a holdup. At the time I thought it was hilarious!

No one had told me that on average it takes a serious free-lance writer *five years* to make his first sale (a statistic I've had quoted endlessly at me ever since). So, with touching naiveté, I mailed off four copies of my masterpiece, one each to the four gun mags I regularly bought and read at the time, including one to Jan Libourel, the editor at Petersen's *Handguns* magazine. Three of those manuscripts disappeared into stygian black holes, never again to be seen by the eyes of man. Jan . . . bought it. I couldn't decide whether to cry or feel numb. He even included a nice, very complimentary letter with the contract for the article. Blew me away! And did wonders for the strength of my new-found writer's wings.

When I tell aspiring writers that I sold the first thing I ever wrote, they look at me like I'm a prince from a far-off land. Made a *big* 150 bucks on the deal. It's funny to note that, even years later, that first article of mine has never been published and, at this late date, probably never will be. But, by God, I got paid for it! I was already learning the free-lance writer's motto: "Did the check clear?"

There was a time in my life when I told myself, "If I could ever read my byline in print on a piece of writing just once, look at it and know that what I'd done was good, then I guess I could die happy." Came the day that I finally got to read those three little words that mean so much, "by Duane Thomas," I felt *really good* for about 10 minutes—and then I asked myself, "Okay, what next?"

So I sat down and wrote another piece, shipped it off to Jan, and he bought that one too! And my third as well. Then my next couple of articles got rejected . . . and I became violently depressed. But I stuck to it, selling damn near everything I wrote to one magazine or another. I sold gun articles as a part-time job for three or four years while I was a soldier, and then I pulled the pin, got out of the Army. Sergeant Thomas hung up his uniform, and I've been making my living as a writer ever since.

(Just as a humorous aside, once when I was talking to Jan Libourel about what it was like to be a paratrooper, he made the comment, "My, I wish I'd spent my youth doing something more manly and exciting! Your time in the Airborne is certainly more impressive than anything I can lay claim to!" And I answered him, quite honestly, "Well, actually, it seems to me you spent your youth a lot more profitably than I did mine. Believe me, if there were any way I could trade *my* Airborne jump wings and Recondo badge for *your* Ph.D. I would do it in a *heartbeat!*")

I remember, early on in my writing career, talking to someone in the gun industry (I only wish I could remember exactly who it was) who seemed absolutely amazed when I told him that I do this as my only source of income. He said, "Aside from the writers who are actually on staff at the magazines, there are probably only half a dozen people in the country who can make a living as full-time gunwriters," the implication of course being that I couldn't possibly make it myself. My reply: "Yeah, well now there's seven."

Years since, I've sold hundreds of articles, primarily to Jan

Libourel at Petersen's. Jan has accused me, on occasion, of feeling a feudal loyalty to him and Petersen's Publishing . . . and he's right! Because it all started for me with that first article, that first sale, lo these many years ago. Whether Jan knows it or not, he gave me my dream, made it possible for me to make my living doing the only work I've ever really wanted to do. And I have to say, the more I have to deal with some other editors within the publishing community, the more I appreciate Jan's willingness to give new writers a shot, his cheerful personality, unfailing helpfulness, and professionalism.

So now you can see why this book is dedicated to:

Jan Michael Libourel
Editor, Petersen's *Handguns* magazine.

If you liked this book, you will also want to read these:

HANDBOOK OF HANDGUNS
A Comprehensive Evaluation of Military, Police, Sporting, and Personal-Defense Pistols
by Timothy J. Mullin

Not since Elmer Keith's classic Sixguns has one book offered so much information on handguns! Here Mullin takes pistols into the 21st century with provocative chapters on modifications, "desperation" weapons, the surplus scene, essential reading, traveling abroad with a handgun, shooting schools and more. 8 1/2 x 11, softcover, photos, 240 pp.   **#HHG**

THE RIGHT TO KEEP AND BEAR ARMS
U.S. Senate Report

This little-known U.S. Senate report is potent ammo for all gun owners interested in the preservation of our right to keep and bear arms. It is proof that the U.S. government itself has studied the meaning of the Second Amendment from all perspectives and concluded that every private citizen has the individual right to own and carry firearms in a peaceful manner. 8 1/2 x 11, softcover, 160 pp.   **#BEAR**

FIREWORKS
A Gunsite Anthology
by Jeff Cooper

Cooper's *Fireworks* is a collection of wild, hilarious, shocking and always meaningful tales from the remarkable life of a firearms legend. Mount up and ride along with Cooper as he fights the Japanese in the Pacific, hunts giant Cape buffalo in Africa, recounts the exploits of such fighting men as Wild Bill Hickock and Medal of Honor winner Col. Herman Henry Hanneken and more. 8 1/2 x 11, softcover, photos, illus.,192pp.   **#WORKS**

TO RIDE, SHOOT STRAIGHT, AND SPEAK THE TRUTH
by Jeff Cooper

Combat mind-set, proper sighting, tactical residential architecture, nuclear war – these are some of the many subjects explored by Jeff Cooper in this illustrated anthology. The author discusses various arms, fighting skills and the importance of knowing how to defend oneself, and one's honor, in our rapidly changing world. 5 1/2 x 8 1/2, soft-cover, illus., 384 pp.   **#RIDE2**

GUNS, BULLETS, AND GUNFIGHTS
Lessons and Tales from a Modern-Day Gunfighter
by Jim Cirillo

Learn what it takes to survive a real gunfight from someone who's been in many – Jim Cirillo, top gun in the New York City Police Department stakeout unit. Read about the stress and intensity of an actual shoot-out and how to maximize your training, ammo and weapons to prevail. 5 1/2 x 8 1/2, softcover, photos, 136 pp.   **#BULLETS**